The
BBC Micro
An Expert Guide

Mike James

Editorial Adviser: Henry Budgett

GRANADA
London Toronto Sydney New York

Granada Publishing Limited – Technical Books Division
Frogmore, St Albans, Herts AL2 2NF
and
36 Golden Square, London W1R 4AH
515 Madison Avenue, New York, NY 10022, USA
117 York Street, Sydney, NSW 2000, Australia
60 International Boulevard, Rexdale, Ontario R9W 6J2, Canada
61 Beach Road, Auckland, New Zealand

British Library Cataloguing in Publication Data
James, Mike
The BBC micro.
1. BBC Microcomputer
I. Title
001.64′04   QA76.8.B3

ISBN 0–246–12014–2

First published in Great Britain 1983 by Granada Publishing

Typeset by V & M Graphics Ltd, Aylesbury, Bucks
Printed in Great Britain by Mackays of Chatham, Kent

Granada ®
Granada Publishing ®

The
BBC Micro
An Expert Guide

Contents

Preface   vii
1   The Hardware   1
2   BBC BASIC   22
3   The Machine Operating System   43
4   The Video Display   54
5   The Sound Generator   76
6   Interfacing   96
7   Introduction to Assembly Language   115
8   Assembly Language II   137
9   Postscript   153
Index   157

Preface

The subject of this book is the BBC Micro, its hardware and its software and it is aimed at anyone who has already started to plumb the depths of this fascinating machine. It is not an introduction to BASIC nor does it attempt to explain the fundamental hardware that goes to make up any computer. Instead it plunges straight into the complexities and intricacies of this very special micro.

The BBC Micro is a complex machine and it would be unreasonable to expect to understand it in one go. To appreciate the working of one part of the machine you have to understand its interaction with other parts and this, of course, implies knowledge of those other parts! Coming to terms with the BBC Micro is, therefore, very like solving a jigsaw puzzle – odd pieces start to make sense, then one or two fit together until the whole jigsaw is finished. The objective of this book is to help you to view the BBC Micro as a whole rather than just a collection of pieces.

Some of the chapters of this book are mainly about hardware and some are mainly about software. If you understand and enjoy hardware then don't give up on the software chapters – they will improve your appreciation of the hardware. Similarly, if you are a programmer, stray outside of your field and see what the hardware is about – you will find that it's not as difficult as it looks! A book of this sort, however, has to assume a certain amount of prior knowledge in its readers. This implies that to understand everything in every chapter you will need to know something about both hardware and software – not very much but something! My advice is to look up any areas that you feel unsure of in a general computer text book.

Material that is covered in the BBC User Guide is, as far as possible, not duplicated here. However, to make the book reasonably self-contained, some repetition has been unavoidable. Where this has happened, the information has been presented in a different way or commented on so as to add something to the User Guide.

The BBC Micro is such an interesting machine that even in a book of this length there must be more left unsaid than said! My apologies to anyone who feels that I have ignored some important feature in preference for something obvious, but choosing what is important is a matter of personal interest and deciding what is obvious is a matter of personal knowledge! My selection is necessarily incomplete and therefore cannot possibly please everybody all of the time.

Finally, let me say that the BBC Micro is, in my opinion, a machine that will be with us when others have decayed back to the sand that their silicon chips came from! It is an excellent machine. It is powerful enough for most applications, it is expandable to respond to the unforeseen needs of the future, and has enough depth to make it a constant source of interest. This must be a winning combination!

Grateful thanks are due to Chris Turner of Acorn, without whose help this book would have lacked many essential pieces of information and to Henry Budgett of *Computing Today* who encouraged me to tackle some of the BBC Micro's challenges. Chapters Four and Five of this book are based on material that first appeared in *Computing Today*.

Mike James

Chapter One
The Hardware

If you have used a BBC Micro for any length of time you will not
have missed the fact that it is a very versatile machine. This
versatility comes in part from its remarkably clever hardware design
and in part from the extensive and well-designed resident software in
the form of BBC BASIC, the assembler and the MOS (Machine
Operating System). Even if your main interest lies in software,
knowing something about the hardware that makes your BBC
Micro 'tick' will help you to get the best from it. This knowledge
needn't be at all detailed. It's not important to know what every chip
does, only what the different general areas do and how they affect
each other, and you can acquire this sort of knowledge even if
electronics is not your subject.

In this chapter we take an overview of the BBC Micro's hardware
by building up a block diagram. Some of the sections of the block
diagram will be explained in more detail in other chapters where
they are discussed in connection with the other side of the story – the
software. Others are examined at length here. If you find any of the
detail tough going then don't despair – simply skip the section or
turn to a more software-oriented chapter and wait until you need to
know about the particular subject that you found difficult before
turning back to this chapter. There are many things inside the BBC
Micro that don't make very much sense until you *need* to know
about them!

The elements of a computer

There is nothing startling about the design of the BBC Micro. You
won't find any powerful new microprocessor inside and its total
memory capacity is limited to a fairly standard 64K bytes. What
makes the design special is not any single component or feature but

the way a range of things have been brought together with a great deal of skill and forethought. The BBC Micro's design is intricate rather than revolutionary.

If you look at Figure 1.1 you will see the parts that every computer, including the BBC Micro, has to have in one form or another to work. Although the BBC Micro adopts this traditional computer pattern there is something special to say about each part.

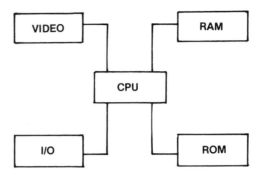

Fig. 1.1. Simplified diagram of the BBC Micro.

The CPU and memory

The CPU (Central Processing Unit) is a 6502 microprocessor of the same type that you will find in many older machines, such as the PET and the APPLE. However, in the case of the BBC Micro it is a double speed device – in other words it operates at 2 MHz. This is a great advantage that isn't wasted by surrounding the fast 6502 with slower memory – everything in the BBC Micro is built for speed! However, it is sometimes necessary for the 6502 to talk to slower devices and to make this possible it can run at half its usual speed – i.e. at 1 MHz.

The RAM is special for the same reason – it is fast. Traditional RAM will allow roughly one memory access every microsecond but the 4816 dynamic RAMs inside the BBC Micro are accessed four times every microsecond. As the 6502 – fast as it is – can only manage to use two of these memory accesses, you might be puzzled why the memory needs to be so fast. For the answer to this mystery we will have to wait for a discussion of the video section. Apart from speed, the 4816 dynamic RAMs are fairly standard 16K bit chips. So, for the Model A you need eight to make 16K bytes and for the Model B you need sixteen chips to make 32K bytes and this is the maximum amount of RAM that can be installed. However, it's far from the maximum amount of memory.

The standard BBC Micro has 32K of ROM in the form of two 16K chips. This is a very large amount of ROM storage by current standards. One of the 16K chips holds a large program known as the MOS (Machine Operating System) which is responsible for co-ordinating the machine's functions and making some of its features easier to use. We will take a more detailed look at the MOS in Chapter Three. Even though the MOS is a large program, it only uses 15K of the 16K. Very little of the remaining 1K of the ROM is used. In fact, most of its address space is given over to memory mapped I/O devices, but this will become a little clearer when we look at the memory map in detail later on in this chapter. The second 16K ROM is most definitely all used as it stores the BBC BASIC interpreter and the 6502 assembler, which are both the subjects of later chapters. What is interesting about this ROM is that it can be replaced by any of three alternative ROMs under software control.

Inside the BBC Micro there are five 16K ROM sockets. One is used for the MOS ROM already discussed and the other four can hold various ROMs. However, only one of these four ROMs can be in use at any one time. For example, suppose one of the sockets held the BBC BASIC ROM (as is the case with nearly all machines) and another held a ROM for another language such as Pascal. Then, by using only software – in other words, without having to dive inside the machine each time – you can select which ROM is to be active and have either BASIC or Pascal. This idea of a number of ROMs sharing the same address space is known as *paging*. By using paging the BBC Micro can have as much as 5×16K (including the MOS) of ROM installed. The range of things that you could put in the four ROMs isn't limited to languages. You could install applications ROMs containing, for example, word processors, accounting packages etc. As well as being able to take 16K ROMs, the four *paged* sockets can also be used with four 4K ROMs to fill the full 16K or with two pairs of 8K ROMs providing only two alternative *fillings* of the 16K. However, these situations are not common.

Switching between any of the four ROMs involves the use of a register at FE30. This register is in fact a *write only device*, i.e. you can use it to change ROMs but not to find out which ROM is selected. If you open your BBC Micro then you will see a row of ROM sockets on the right-hand side of the edge nearest the keyboard. As mentioned earlier, most systems will have only two of the sockets filled. The one on the far left contains the MOS and the one next to it contains the BBC BASIC. If you number the ROM sockets starting with the one that holds BBC BASIC as ROM 0 then you can select the ROM of your choice by writing its number to the register. So, if you want to select BBC BASIC, write zero to the register. If you want to select the ROM in the socket to the immediate right of the BASIC ROM, then you have to write a 1 to the register. This all sounds easy enough but beware that the ROM that you are *deselecting* isn't necessary for your program to run. In other words, don't deselect the BASIC ROM from a BASIC program!

The video section

The video section of the BBC Micro is perhaps the most interesting of all. Its workings will be examined in some detail in Chapter Four but it is worth sketching out its overall configuration here. The information to be displayed on the TV screen is stored in the machine's RAM. In display modes 0–6 the dot pattern for the entire display is stored in RAM. In other words every dot displayed on the screen is stored in the RAM. However, in mode 7 only, the ASCII code for each character displayed on the screen is stored in memory. The actual dot patterns that make up the shapes of the characters on the screen are stored in an additional ROM that is inaccessible to the 6502 and is used only in mode 7. Most computers produce their video display in the same way that the BBC Micro produces its mode 7 display.

There are two main parts to the video section – a standard 6845 video generator, and a very special custom-made chip called the video processor. The video generator chip shares access to the RAM with the 6502 processor; it uses the two memory accesses per microsecond that the 6502 cannot (see the previous section on the CPU). Thus, in every microsecond the memory access sequence is:

6502, video generator, 6502, video generator

The video generator has access to the RAM for the simple reason that this is where the information to be displayed is stored. However, the video generator doesn't handle or process any of this information – this task is reserved for the video processor! What it actually does is to generate the correct sequence of addresses at the correct time, to ensure that the RAM gives up its information in the correct order and at the correct time. It has other jobs to do as well but they are all connected in some way with timing and organisation. For example, the video generator produces the regular part of the video signal in the form of line and frame sync pulses. The data that the RAM produces as a result of being addressed by the video generator is not at all suitable for direct conversion into a video signal. For one thing, it is produced eight bits at a time whereas a video signal needs one bit at a time. For another, the video signal needs colour information and this is coded within the eight bits. As already mentioned, the chip that takes the outputs from RAM and turns it into a video signal is the video processor chip. This not only converts the eight bits coming from memory into a serial stream but also decodes the colour information to produce a standard RGB (Red, Green, Blue) colour output. However, in mode 7 the video processor does very little. The ASCII codes stored in memory are fed directly to the character generator ROM which produces a standard RGB output all on its own!

The video section is a little complicated so it is worth summarising all the information in the form of a black diagram (see Figures 1.2 and 1.3). This thumbnail sketch of the way the graphics section of the BBC Micro works will be extended considerably in Chapter Four so don't worry too much if you find yourself wondering about the details. All will be revealed later!

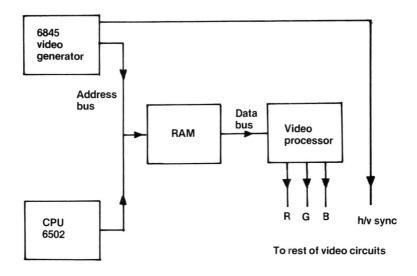

Fig. 1.2. Simplified block diagram of video section in modes 0–6.

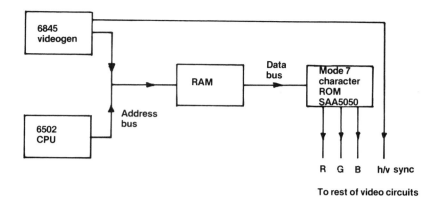

Fig. 1.3. Simplified block diagram of video sections in mode 7.

The interfaces

This is in fact a heading under which to gather together a wide range of different circuits! Some of these, such as the sound generator, the user port and the A to D convertor, for example, are dealt with at length in other chapters but it is worth producing a summary of all the interfaces circuits inside a standard BBC Micro. One thing that all the interface circuits have in common is that they use the 1K of address space not used by the MOS ROM.

The interfacing circuits within a standard Model A BBC Micro are:

1. Cassette and RS423 serial.
2. VIA (Versatile Interface Adaptor)–A. This is a parallel interface looking after internal devices such as the keyboard and the sound generator.
3. The 1 MHz extension bus.
4. The tube.

In the standard Model B machine we have to add:

5. VIA-B – a parallel interface that looks after two external ports, the centronics printer and the user port.
6. An A to D convertor (a μPD7002) that can be used as a general purpose measuring device or with joysticks.

There are other interface circuits that can be added to the BBC Micro beyond even these six, such as the disc interface, but these are of less general interest and will be discussed in Chapter Nine. We will now take a look at each of the above interfaces, apart from the A to D convertor which is dealt with in detail in Chapter Six and is so separate that it adds little to our understanding of the overall machine.

The cassette and RS423 interface

Every BBC Micro comes equipped with a cassette interface. The interface also doubles as a general purpose serial interface. It is true that owners of the Model A cannot use this serial interface but this is only because the two buffer chips that provide the power to drive the serial output to the RS243 standard are missing. (The RS243 standard is simply an improved version of the older and better known RS232 or V24 standards. For our purpose it may be considered entirely compatible with both.)

The cassette interface on the BBC Micro relies on two major components. The first is a 6850 ACIA (AsynChronous Interface Adaptor) which is responsible for changing data from a parallel to a serial format and vice versa. This is all that is necessary for the RS243 interface (apart from the aforementioned buffering). However, the cassette interface works by recording two audio tones corresponding to the binary zeros and ones in the serial bit stream

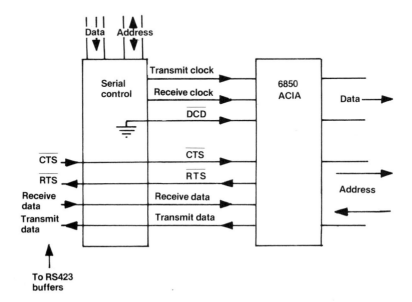

Fig. 1.4. Serial interface set-up for RS423.

produced by the 6850 ACIA. It is the second of the major chips in the cassette interface that is responsible for changing audio tones to bits. This is the second custom-made chip (the first being the video processor) in the BBC Micro. As well as changing bits to tones and tones to bits, it is responsible for providing the clock signals that determine how fast the ACIA receives and transmits (i.e. it sets the baud rate) and it selects where the ACIA should take its inputs and output from – the cassette or the RS423 buffers.

The simplest configuration is when the interface is set up to *drive* the RS423 serial port. In this case the only thing that the custom *serial control* chip does is to generate the transmit and receive clocks, and pass on all the input to and output from the 6850 ACIA. You can see this in Figure 1.4. To help anyone interested in using the RS423 interface the following table describes the function of each of the ACIA signals:

ACIA *signal*		*Function*
$\overline{\text{DCD}}$	(No carrier)	Not used on the BBC Micro's RS423 interface.
$\overline{\text{CTS}}$	(Not clear to send)	A signal *to* the BBC Micro indicating when it is OK for it to send data.
$\overline{\text{RTS}}$	(Not ready to send)	A signal *from* the BBC Micro indicating that it is ready to receive data.

Connecting a printer, or anything else, to the RS423 port is very often a matter of getting the receive and transmit rates correct and deciding what, if anything, to connect to the control signals. The BBC Micro's side of the control signals is simple enough. To drive a printer the only two signals required are *transmit data* and *clear to send* (CTS). However, depending on which of the many available printers is used, the printer may need rather more signals than this to actually print anything! This is governed by the details of the printer's hardware, which should be explained in its documentation.

The situation is a little more complicated when the interface is set up to drive the cassette. In this case most of the ACIA's signals are intercepted by the serial controller. This can be seen in Figure 1.5. When recording data the serial controller switches on the cassette motor and then synthesises sine waves of the correct frequencies as the serial data is fed to it from the ACIA. The only ACIA control line used in recording is the *ready to send* (RTS) line which enables (i.e. switches on and off) the tone generator. The recording rate is set

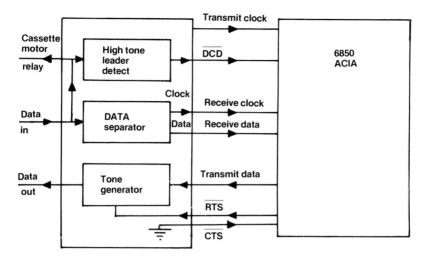

Fig. 1.5. Serial interface set-up for cassette.

by the frequency of the transmit clock. On playback, things are just a little more complicated. First, the high continuous tone (2400 Hz for 5 seconds) is detected by a special circuit, the *high tone leader detect*. When this is detected, the *data carrier detect* (DCD) line is set to enable the ACIA to receive data. That is, before the high tone is detected the ACIA will not accept any data that might be coming from the tape and hence through the serial controller. The main part of the playback circuit, however, is the *data separator*. This accepts the recorded tones from the tape recorder and changes them into a stream of zeros and ones suitable for the ACIA to convert to a parallel form. As well as detecting whether the input tone is high or low, the data separator generates a clock signal that is used as the receive clock to the ACIA. The advantage of this is that it takes into account any changes in tape speed that might have occurred between recording and playback.

This description of how the serial interface works is all very well but how do you select which of the cassette or the RS423 interface is to be active? How do you select the transmit and receive rates? The answers to these questions depend on knowing about certain control registers in the interface area of memory. The serial interface has three control registers – two belong to the ACIA and one belongs to the serial controller. The addresses where these and other registers can be found are given in the section below on the BBC Micro's memory map but for the sake of completeness the addresses and functions of each register are given below:

Address *(in Hex)*	*Function*
FE08	ACIA control and status.
FE09	ACIA receive and transmit;
FE10	Serial controller's register.

The two ACIA registers are rather strange in that their function depends on whether you are reading or writing them. For example, the register at FE08 is a control register when you write to it and a status register when you read it! If you think about it this makes a great deal of sense – why should you want to read a control register and write a status register? The function of the bits in the ACIA's control register can be seen in Figure 1.6. For normal use, bits

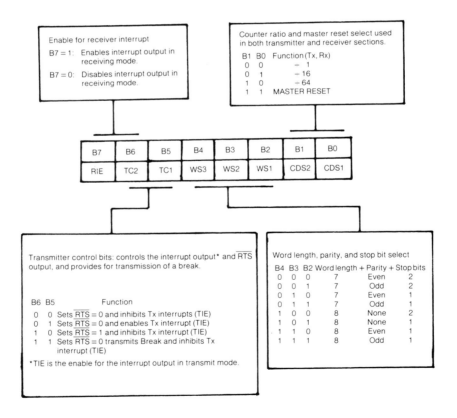

Fig. 1.6. ACIA Control Register format.

7,6,5,1 and 0 should be left as the BBC Micro sets them, i.e. use the appropriate FX commands to set the baud rates and generally initialise the register. The only bits that might need altering are bits 4,3 and 2 to set the required serial word format (for more information, see the VDU example in Chapter Eight). The meaning of the bits in the ACIA's status register can be seen in Figure 1.7. The

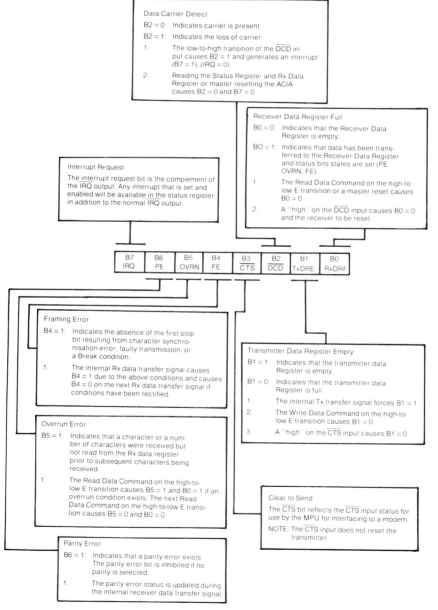

Fig. 1.7. The ACIA Status Register format.

data transmit and receive registers can be read and written as required. If bit 0 of the status register is 1 this means that the receive register contains a character which should be read before the next character is received and hence overwrites it. If bit 1 of the status register is 1 a character may be placed in the transmit register to be transmitted bit by bit. If bit 1 is 0 then you shouldn't write anything to the transmit register because this would overwrite the character currently being transmitted. The other bits in the status register are concerned either with telling the user about errors that have occurred or with the status of the external device.

The final register of interest is the serial control register and its format can be seen in Figure 1.8. Bit 7 controls the cassette motor

Bit 7	Bit 6	Bit 5	Bit 4	Bit 3	Bit 2	Bit 1	Bit 0
CM	RS423/Cass	Receive Rate			Transmit Rate		

Fig. 1.8 The serial control register.

relay. If it is 1 then the relay is closed and the motor is on. To see this, try ?&FE10=&80 which will switch the motor on and ?&FE10=0 which will switch it off again. Bit 6 controls which of the cassette or the RS423 interface is selected – 0 selects the cassette and a 1 selects the RS423. The final six bits work in two groups of three to control the baud rate for receive and transmit. These work as indicated in Table 1.1 below.

Table 1.1. Baud rates produced by bit patterns in the serial control register.

Baud rate	Receive bit 3 4 5	Transmit bit 0 1 2
75	1 1 1	1 1 1
150	1 1 0	1 1 0
300	1 0 1	1 0 1
1200	1 0 0	1 0 0
2400	0 1 1	0 1 1
4800	0 1 0	0 1 0
9600	0 0 1	0 0 1
19200	0 0 0	0 0 0

Notice that the order of the bits is the reverse of what you would normally expect.

A lot of information has been introduced in this section without an example of how to use it. This is because direct access to the serial interface is best done via the 6502 assembler and this is not discussed until Chapters Seven and Eight. If you cannot wait that long, turn to Chapter Eight where you will find a program that turns the BBC Micro into a VDU making use of much of the information in this section.

The VIAs

A fully expanded machine contains two VIAs (Versatile Interface Adaptors). VIA-A is used for internal tasks and VIA-B is dedicated to user-defined tasks. A VIA is fundamentally a parallel interface but it has many other functions and capabilities. For example, it contains two independent timers and a serial shift register. In fact it rivals the 6502 itself in its complexity! Because it is such a complicated and versatile device a large part of Chapter Six is devoted to it. As Chapter Six is mostly concerned with VIA-B, the user's VIA, it is worth taking a brief look at what VIA-A is doing. Without knowledge of how a VIA works this is necessarily an incomplete description but the information in Chapter Six rounds off the picture.

VIA-A is used by the BBC Micro to interface the keyboard, the sound generator, the A to D convertor, and the optional light pen, and VIA-A's timer is used by BASIC to provide the variable TIME. It is also used to handle *hardware scrolling*, a topic which is dealt with in Chapter Four. There are two ten-bit ports in every VIA, usually referred to as *port A* and *port B*. Eight bits of each port can be individually selected to be either inputs or outputs. The remaining two bits are a little more restricted in their use and are normally kept for special purposes. The A side of the VIA handles the keyboard and the B side handles the 'odds and ends'.

The keyboard is connected to the eight data bits on port A. One of the two special bits – CA2 – is also used to detect when a key is pressed. The keyboard has two modes of operation – free-running and program-controlled. When the keyboard is free-running, each key is repeatedly scanned in turn until a key is pressed when a signal (an interrupt) is sent by CA2 to the 6502. This causes the 6502 to stop whatever it is doing and 'pay attention' to the keyboard. When this happens, the keyboard is switched to its programmed mode of operation and the keys are scanned one by one, using the eight A side data lines until the key that is pressed is found. To understand this a little more fully you have to know the layout of the keyboard, which is presented in Figure 1.9. Being arranged into a matrix consisting

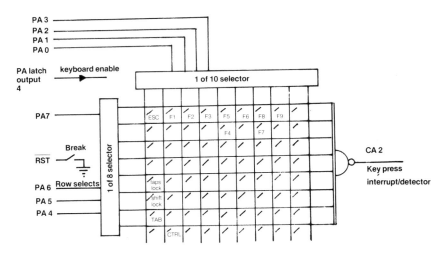

Fig. 1.9. The keyboard in program mode.

of 10 columns by 8 rows means that any column can be selected using four bits and any row can be selected using three bits. The column number is specified using bits 0–3 and the row number is specified using bits 4–6 (see Figure 1.9). In addition, bit 7 is used to control access to the keyboard. The second special bit on the A side of the VIA is connected to the vertical sync signal for timing purposes. The important thing to notice from this description of the keyboard is that, as the keyboard causes an interrupt every time a key is pressed, keyboard service can occur at any time. In particular the ESCAPE key is just like any other key, i.e. it doesn't use any special *reset* function – in this sense any key could be used to interrupt program operation. However, the BREAK key is connected to the 6502's reset line and is different from the other keys, causing a hardware reset when it is pressed. It is possible, however, for the machine to tell the difference between a reset that occurs when the machine is first switched on – a *cold reset* – and a reset caused by pressing the BREAK key – a *warm reset*. This distinction allows the machine to decide whether it is worth taking any notice of the memory contents, in particular user-definable key definitions.

Even though it is different from the other nine function keys, this means that the BREAK key can be associated with a *KEY definition. The BREAK key always causes a reset but, following a warm reset, the machine obeys any instructions assigned to *KEY 10, i.e. the BREAK key.

The B side of the VIA has a number of jobs to do. The two special bits CB1 and CB2 are used to detect the end of conversion of the A to D convertor and a signal from the optional light pen respectively. Bits 0 to 3 are fed into a 74LS259 addressable latch which provides eight different outputs. The first three bits, i.e. 0 to 2, determine which output from the latch is affected. Thus, 000 alters the first output, 001 alters the second ouput, and so on. Bit 3 determines the state that the selected output takes. That is, if bit 3 is 1 the selected output changes to 1. To describe what the latch does involves describing the effect of each output. The first output enables the 75489 sound generator. The second and third are connected to the optional speech synthesiser. The fourth is used to enable the keyboard, i.e. to load column and row numbers. The fifth and sixth are used in the hardware scrolling and are set according to the display mode that the BBC Micro is in. The seventh and eighth drive the caps lock and shift lock LEDs. What is interesting is the way the latch is used to select any combination of a number of devices. The sound generator chip and the optional speech synthesiser are both connected to the A side data bits 0 to 7. You can think of the A data side as a *slow data bus* communicating with whichever device is selected by the addressable latch. This means that only one of keyboard, sound generator and speech synthesiser can be activated at any one time. The final four bits of side B are used a little more simply. Bits 4 and 5 are used as 'fire button' inputs from the analog connector. Bits 6 and 7 are used to control the optional speech synthesiser.

This just about finishes the description of VIA-A (for a summary see Figure 1.10) – except to remind the reader that it also provides the timing function for the BASIC variable TIME. (In fact it uses timer 1 but this will be explained in Chapter Six).

The 1 MHz bus

The 1 MHz bus is not so much an interface, but is more a way of connecting other interfaces to the BBC Micro. The reason why it is called the '1 MHz' bus is that the speed at which the 6502 normally

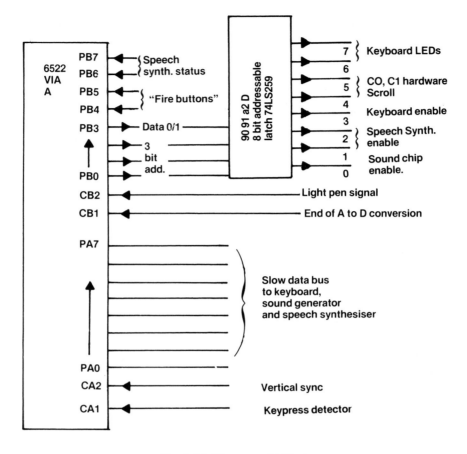

Fig. 1.10. The use of VIA-A.

works, i.e. 2 MHz, is too fast for most standard components so the clock which governs the speed of access is slowed to 1 MHz when the 6502 is using addresses that correspond to the 1 MHz bus.

The bus itself isn't a collection of all the address and control lines that the BBC Micro uses internally, as is the case with the expansion buses of most other micros. Instead it only includes the full data bus, the eight low address lines A0–A7, and a few control lines. The presence of A0 to A7 means that the bus can specify any one of ¼K of address locations – but which address locations? If you are looking only at the low eight bits of the address then 0045, say, looks exactly the same as 3545, because the low eight address bits are the same in both cases. To solve this problem, the 1 MHz bus includes two extra addressing lines – NPGFC and NPGFD. These are normally high, at logic 1, but if an address beginning with FC is used NPGFC goes low and if an address beginning with FD is used NPGFD goes low. You might be able to see now why these two lines have such long names – NPGFC stands for 'not page FC' and NPGFD stands for 'not page FD'! Obviously, if you connect anything to the 1 MHz bus and use a combination of NPGFC and A0–A7 to enable it, it has an address in the range FC00 to FCFF. If you use NPGFD and A0–A7 then it has an address in the region FD00 to FDFF. What this means is that you can connect external devices, running at 1 MHz to the BBC Micro, using either of the above range of addresses. However, Acorn have already suggested uses for most of this address space in their *Application Note No. 1 – The 1 MHz Bus* which can be obtained from Acorn. Only addresses between FCC0 to FCFE are marked for 'user application' but this should be enough for most purposes.

This short sketch of the 1 MHz bus in insufficient if you are interested in connecting your own equipment to the BBC Micro. In particular be warned that there is a slight timing problem to be solved before any equipment will work reliably. Details of this and other features of the 1 MHz bus can be found in the *Application Note* mentioned above which should be obtained by anyone considering interfacing to the 1 MHz bus.

The tube

The tube interface is superficially like the 1 MHz bus in that it supplies a subset of the address lines – A0 to A6 and an extra address line called *the tube*. There are two differences, however. First, the tube works at the full 2 MHz and secondly it is claimed for exclusive use by Acorn products. There is no real reason why the tube couldn't be used as a fast version of the 1 MHz bus but it is likely to be of much more use as originally intended. For one thing, Acorn have produced a custom chip that can be used to pass data between the 6502 in the BBC Micro and other processors very quickly and in a standard format. Using only seven address lines means that the tube can only be used to address 128 distinct locations. The tube address control, when used in combination with A0–A6, places the tube at FEE0 to FEFF.

The whole machine – a block diagram and the memory map

After studying the various parts of the BBC Micro you should be able to make something of Figure 1.11 which shows the areas of the machine in roughly the same position that they are placed on the printed circuit board. Some of the extra devices, such as the disc controller and the speech synthesiser, have been left out for clarity.

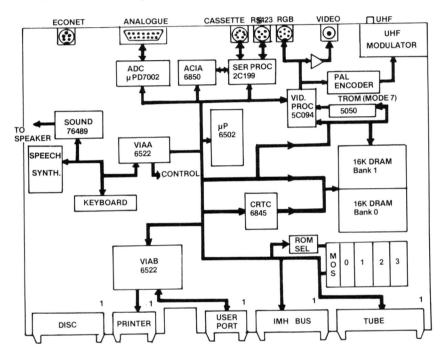

Fig. 1.11. Complete block diagram.

It is also worth drawing together all the information on the position of various things in memory. A complete memory map can be seen in Figure 1.12. The RAM area (16K or 32K depending on model) is used for general system storage, BASIC programs, and the screen displays. More details will be given of RAM usage in the relevant chapters. Notice the four paged ROMs starting at 8000; remember that only one is actually present in the memory at any one time and that which one it is is controlled by the ROM select latch. The area of greatest interest is the 1K I/O area at the top of the memory. This can be seen in greater detail in Figure 1.13. The lower ½K of this area is used by devices connected to the 1 MHz expansion

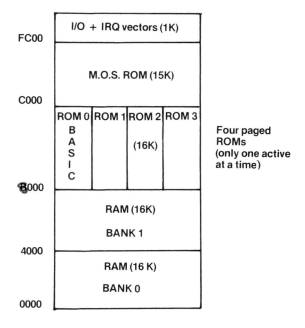

Fig. 1.12. Complete memory map.

bus, as was described earlier. The 128 bytes starting at FE00 are used by internal I/O devices, many of which have already been discussed. The addresses given on the left hand side are the start addresses of any registers that the device might have. The details of the control and status registers of each device will be given in the chapters where they are discussed more fully. The exceptions are the FDC – Floppy Disc Controller – and the ADLC – Advanced Data Link Controller – which are not part of the standard BBC machine. Notice that the details of the serial controller and the ROM select have been given in this chapter.

Knowing about hardware

If you know the details of the hardware of a particular computer then the temptation is to make use of it! In other words, once you know about hardware, easy ways of doing things and even new things to do often occur to you. Now with most machines this is a very acceptable way to proceed but with the BBC Micro there has to be a note of caution. The BBC Micro is intended to be the start of a

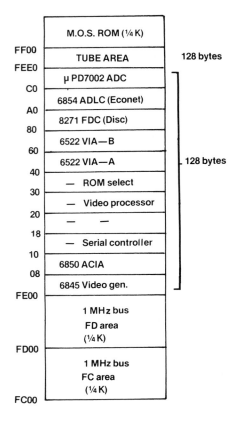

Fig. 1.13. I/O area of memory.

very advanced system. In particular the tube can be used to connect other processors. If you have written a program that runs on a standard BBC Micro by directly 'fiddling' with the hardware, then this program is *hardware-dependent*. If the design of the BBC Micro changes, even slightly, then the chances are your program will not work. In particular, your program will not work on a second processor connected over the tube. This may, however, not worry you too much. After all, if the program works on your BBC Micro, why worry? However, it is something to keep in mind when producing programs that you hope will be useful to other people.

To help with this problem, the BBC Micro's MOS provides a number of standard routines to enable you to modify memory and I/O locations. In addition there are also routines that provide standard ways of dealing with the internal devices. Acorn suggest that if these routines are used intead of direct access to the device or location then your programs will run on a modified BBC Micro, even on the second processor! You will find an example of using the MOS to deal with I/O devices in Chapter Six.

A second point to be aware of, and perhaps even beware of, is that the BBC Micro makes extensive use of interrupts in its operation. This makes it a much faster and more flexible machine but it can make it more difficult to program at the machine code level if you need to make use of interrupts yourself.

Conclusion

This chapter has presented an overview of the BBC Micro's hardware and looked in detail at some of the features that are not covered extensively in later chapters. Don't worry if you have found parts of this chapter hard to assimilate. Looked at in isolation, hardware is difficult to understand unless you are well-versed in electronics. In some ways, this chapter is meant to be treated as a reference section and you'll find the information it contains will become much easier to understand when you encounter a situation that actually requires it. So if you carry on exploring aspects of the BBC Micro for yourself you'll find yourself returning to this chapter time and again.

Chapter Two
BBC BASIC

Not only is the BBC Micro a remarkable and interesting machine from the hardware point of view, it also has some equally impressive software. One of the interesting characteristics of the software is the way that it interacts with the hardware to produce something that is extremely versatile. For example, the sound generator chip is fairly sophisticated in that it has three tone channels and a noise channel, but when you add in the ENVELOPE command it behaves in a way that seems to exceed its specification! Much of the way that the sound generator appears to the user is entirely the invention of well-conceived software. In this chapter we look at BBC BASIC which forms roughly half of the resident software in the machine. (The other half, the MOS, is considered in Chapter Three.)

Rather than going through a point-by-point discussion of the commands that make up the BASIC, a task already accomplished by the User Guide, the first part of this chapter looks at some of the features and commands that either make BBC BASIC special or are in some way difficult or unusual. In the second half of the chapter we take a look inside and find out how the BASIC interpreter runs and stores your BASIC programs. This sort of information is often interesting and is worth knowing for its own sake. Also, there are many practical reasons for delving into the interpreter. Knowing how the BASIC is implemented can suggest the fastest and most economical ways of doing things. It can also suggest 'short cuts' and ways of accomplishing what would otherwise be impossible (for example, printing a list of all the variables in use). Finally, the assembly language programmer needs to know something of how variables are stored in order to make use of the parameter-passing capabilities of the CALL statement (see Chapters Seven and Eight).

BBC BASIC, a BASIC with structure

When Acorn were approached by the BBC to produce a computer, one of the specifications was that its BASIC should include statements not normally thought of as being part of the language. The reason for this was the desire to make BASIC a more academically respectable language and to make it able to take advantage of the method of programming known as 'structured programming'. The theory behind this method of programming is not within the scope of this book but its practical interpretation has come to mean the use of the commands:

IF ... THEN ... ELSE
REPEAT ... UNTIL
WHILE ... DO ...
and
FOR ..=.. TO ..

BBC BASIC doesn't include all of these statements; it lacks WHILE, but even so it can claim to be a 'structured BASIC'. If you want to treat BBC BASIC like an ordinary BASIC, that is programming using only IF ... THEN, GOTO and FOR, then you can. However, if you want to write BASIC in a structured way there is more to it than just adding the more complete form of the IF and the REPEAT ... UNTIL statement to your repertoire. It is the aim of structured programming to produce programs that are easy to undertstand and as bug-free as possible and this can be achieved in many ways. The most important thing is to try and make the 'flow of control' through your program as simple and obvious as possible. You can do this by restricting the way that you use GOTO, by using REPEAT ... UNTIL and FOR to form loops in preference to GOTO and by using subroutines to group statements together into logical units. To go into any more detail about structured programming would take us far from our subject. If this brief introduction has whet your appetite then you can find out more about structured programming and good programming style in general from my other book, *The Complete Programmer*. However, it is worth looking at the subject of subroutines a little more.

Subroutines, procedures and functions

One of the biggest criticisms of BASIC is that it has a very limited ability to group statements together into logical units. True, you can use GOSUB and RETURN to form subroutines but this has a number of shortcomings, as follows:

1. You have to refer to subroutines by a line number rather than a name that indicates the subroutine's purpose.
2. Subroutines and the rest of the program have unrestricted access to each other's variables.
3. There is no way to isolate the variables that supply inputs to and return results from a subroutine – in other words there are no facilities for parameters.

The first problem can be overcome to a certain extent by assigning the line number to an appropriately named variable. For example, if you wanted to call a subroutine starting at line 2000 that sorted an array into order, instead of:

GOSUB 2000

you could use

SORT = 2000
GOSUB SORT

However, this technique makes renumbering a program very difficult. You may not see why the second point is a problem. Why shouldn't a program and a subroutine share the same variables? There are a number of valid arguments to suggest they should not. As subroutines should be collections of statements that carry out identifiable tasks, they are often written without reference to the rest of the program. For example, a subroutine that sorts an array into order is generally useful and might find its way into a number of programs. When writing such a subroutine, what names should you give to the variables that you use so that they don't 'clash' with variables used for other purposes in the main program and other subroutines? Variables clashing in this way is a very common cause of BASIC programs failing to work as expected. If you do have a way of isolating the variables in a subroutine from the rest of the program then the third problem comes into play. If subroutines cannot have access to the variables in the main program how do they receive their input values and return their results? The solution to this problem is, of course, to use parameters in the same way as in a standard BASIC function. In fact, in many respects, the standard BASIC function would be superior to the BASIC subroutine if it were extended to allow more than one statement. This is indeed the direction that BBC BASIC takes in improving the subroutine.

A user-defined function in BBC BASIC can take the 'one line' form found in most other versions of BASIC. For example.

DEF FNsum(a,b,c) = a + b + c

is a function that adds three numbers together. The three parameters a,b and c are not variables in the usual sense of the word in that they do not 'appear' in the main program because they have been used in the function. There is even no problem if the main program uses variables with the same names. In some senses the names used for parameters are only relevant within the function definition. In other words, parameters are *local* to the function. Another thing to notice is that a function returns a single value as a result. It is this that makes it possible to use functions within arithmetic expressions. From the point of view of evaluating expressions, a function behaves just like an ordinary variable except that the value associated with its name is produced by the function rather than just stored in memory. However, even though this is a very useful feature there are many occasions when a subroutine needs to return more than a single result.

BBC BASIC improves the standard BASIC function to allow multiple statements in its definition. For example, it is possible to write a function that finds the larger of two numbers:

```
100  DEF FNmax(a,b)
110  ans=a
120  IF a<b THEN ans=b
130  =ans
```

Line 100 states that what follows is the definition of a function called FNmax. Lines 110 and 120 place the larger of a and b and place the result in ans. Perhaps the oddest looking line is 130. Multi-line functions always end with an assignment with no variable on the left-hand side. The effect of this is to set the value returned by the function to the result of the expression on the right of the equals sign. Once the value of the function has been determined it is used in the evaluation of the expression in which the function occurred in the main program. Once again it is useful to think of this last assignment statement as *storing* the result of the function in a *dummy* variable with the same name as the function. The parameters a and b are, again, local to the function. But, what about the variable ans? This is declared within the function so you might expect it to 'belong' to the function. In fact it is a variable that is part of the rest of the program. The variable ans is no different from any other variable in a standard BASIC program. This is something of a disadvantage if there is already a variable ans in use in the main program. If this is the case and FNmax is used then the variable will change its value even if its use in the main program has nothing to do with finding the maximum of two numbers. Such changes caused by functions in *innocent* variables in the main program are called the *side effects* of the function. If you want to write programs that are not only easy to understand but easy to debug then the functions used in your programs shouldn't cause any side effects. BBC BASIC provides the LOCAL statement for just this reason. A variable that is declared in a LOCAL statement behaves much like a parameter in that it has nothing to do with any variables of the same name used in the rest of the program. For example, the FNmax function can be written as:

```
100 DEF FNmax(a,b)
110 LOCAL ans
120 ans=a
130 IF a<b THEN ans=b
140 =ans
```

Now the variable ans is declared as local by line 110 and, just as the names a and b have nothing to do with the main program, the value of ans may be changed without affecting any variable in the main program. This version of FNmax has no side effects! We will consider how parameters and local variables actually work later on in this chapter. However, it is worth pointing out that if you use a parameter or declare a local variable that does not have a counterpart with the same name in the main program then one comes into being as soon as the function is used. (Numeric variables are given the initial value zero and string variables are set to the null string.)

Functions are very useful but they do have the drawback that they can only return one result (excluding side effects). BBC BASIC provides an additional feature – the *procedure* – that is supposed to get around this problem. If you want to return anything other than a single result you should use a procedure. Procedures are a very useful feature of BBC BASIC but the one thing they do not solve is the problem of returning more than one result! In fact there is no clean way of getting any results back from a procedure. A procedure is defined in much the same way as a function but it ends with ENDPROC. For example,

```
10 DEF PROCmaxmin(a,b)
20 IF a>b THEN max=a:min=b ELSE max=b:min=a
30 ENDPROC
```

Line 10 defines the procedure maxmin with two parameters a and b. Line 20 does all the work by placing the two results correctly in the variables max and min. The final line simply marks the end of the procedure in the same way that RETURN ends a subroutine. The two parameters are local in the same way that the parameters in a function are. However, the only way that the two results can be communicated back to the main program is by the use of two non-local variables max and min. As these are non-local, any variables of the same name in the main program will be altered by the use of the procedure. In this sense the only way that a procedure can return any results is by making use of side effects! Any variables used in a procedure that are used purely for internal purposes should be named in a LOCAL statement in an attempt to minimise unnecessary side effects but, unless no results are to be returned, procedures must produce side effects.

Even though procedures have this fundamental shortcoming they are extremely useful – so much so that they are always to be preferred to the standard BASIC subroutine. Although there is much written in the User Guide it is worth highlighting a number of important points concerning functions and procedures:

1. Use a function whenever a single result is to be produced.
2. Place *all* the variables used in a function in a LOCAL statement to remove all side effects.
3. All input to functions and procedures should be via parameters whenever possible.
4. Use a procedure if no results or more than one result is to be produced.
5. In a procedure, name all variables not used to return results in a LOCAL statement to remove unnecessary side effects.
6. Parameters can be any of the three simple variables – real, integer or string – but not an array. Arrays can only be passed as non-local variables.
7. Functions can return strings as results.
8. Functions and procedures are always to be preferred to BASIC subroutines and should be used as often as possible. One good reason is that procedure calls are faster than subroutine calls.
9. The variables used in a procedure or function are only created after the function or procedure is first used.

10. Functions and procedures work slightly faster the second time they are used.
11. Functions and procedures can be called recursively.

The reasoning behind many of these points will become clear as the chapter progresses. However, the final point is worth illustrating with an example. Whenever a function or procedure is called it creates a completely new set of local variables. This fact means that a function or procedure can call itself, i.e. can be used recursively. Recursion is a subject that is dealt with extensively in many an academic textbook. Most people find it difficult to cope with and it is therefore fortunate that it is rarely actually needed in the solution of practical problems. As an example of recursion consider the problem of writing a function to calculate n! (n factorial). The usual way to write a function that calculates n! is by using a FOR loop. (n! is the product of all the integers from 1 to n, that is:

$$n*(n-1)*(n-2)*.....*1$$

from 1 to n).

```
100 DEF FNF(N)
110 LOCAL I,SUM
120 SUM=1
130 FOR I=1 TO N
140 SUM=SUM*I
150 NEXT I
160 =SUM
```

The FOR loop at lines 130 to 150 calculates a *running product* in SUM that is equal to N!.

There is another way to approach the problem of calculating factorials. If you want to know what n! is you could find out by calculating (n−1)! and multiplying it by n. In other words, n!=n*(n−1)!. For example, 4!=4*3!=4*3*2!=4*3*2*1! and we know that 1! is 1. This idea results in the following function:

```
100 DEF FNF(N)
110 IF N<>1 THEN =N*FNF(N-1)
120 =1
```

Line 110 looks very strange in that the expression to the right of the equals sign uses the function FNF. To see how this works follow through the calculation of FNF(3). When FNF is first called, the value of N is 3 so the expression following line 110 is carried out. This involves calling FNF once more but with the value of the parameter N equal to 2. Remember that when FNF is called for the second time a completely new set of variables is created. This second call to FNF also results in FNF being called again but this time with a parameter value of 1, which causes this third call to FNF to finish via line 120. This results in the value 1 being returned as the result of the third call which allows the evaluation of the expression in the second call to be completed i.e. 2*1 and the result passed back to the first call to FNF. Finally, this result allows the expression in the first call to FNF to be completed giving the correct answer 3*2*1.

If this description has left you feeling confused then you are not alone! It is possible to follow the execution of the function through all its 'incarnations' but you really need pencil and paper to do it easily. Recursion is something that you either feel comfortable with or find difficult. You can write recursive functions and procedures in BBC BASIC. However, because procedures do not return results except via non-local variables they are much more limited in the way they can be used recursively.

Indirection and hexadecimal

The provision of REPEAT ... UNTIL functions and procedures certainly make BBC BASIC a 'higher' level language than standard BASIC. However, there are one or two extra facilities included in BBC BASIC that makes it easier to use for lower level tasks. In particular, there are three 'indirection' operators that make the direct manipulation of memory easy.

Most versions of BASIC provide the POKE command to alter a memory location and the PEEK function to examine the contents of a memory location. BBC BASIC replaces both of these facilities by a single indirection operator '?'. Writing a question mark in front of a number or a variable causes it to be interpreted as the address of a single memory location. So, for example, ?40 is a reference to memory location 40. To find out what is in a memory location all you have to do is use PRINT ?address. To change the contents of a memory location you simply write ?address=new value. If you read the question mark as 'the memory location whose address is' then you should be able to understand any use of the indirection operator.

Although it is useful to be able to handle single memory locations the BBC Micro tends to work with more than one location at a time. For example, it uses four memory locations to store an integer. To make the manipulation of multiple memory locations easier two

other indirection operators, ! and $ are available. The exclamation
mark works in the same way as the question mark but it refers to
four memory locations. To be exact the statement !address refers to
the four memory locations whose addresses are address, address+1,
address+2 and address+3. These four locations are treated as if they
were a standard integer value (with the most significant byte stored
in address+3). The dollar sign $ is a little more difficult to
understand in that the number of memory locations that it refers to
is variable. It is known as the *string indirection* operator, because it
deals with memory in terms of strings of characters. For example,
$4000="ABCD" stores the ASCII codes for A in memory location
4000, the code for B in 4001 and so on until it stores the code for D in
memory location 4003. To mark the end of the string it then stores
the ASCII code for carriage return in 4004. In the same way PRINT
$4000 will print the character corresponding to the ASCII codes
stored in the memory locations starting at 4000 and going on up to
the first occurrence of the ASCII code for carriage return.

You can specify an *offset* with any of the three indirection
operators. For example, 4000?10 refers to memory location 4010. In
other words, address?offset is the same as ?(address+offset). This is
a useful facility for *stepping* through a range of addresses but it can
be confusing for the beginner.

The indirection operators certainly provide a way of handling
memory locations but both memory addresses and memory
contents are usually specified in terms of hexadecimal rather than
decimal. The main reasons for this are that you can specify a
memory address using four hex digits and the contents of a memory
location using only two hex digits. BBC BASIC is capable of
handling numbers written in hex and printing values in hex. Writing
'&' in front of a constant indicates that it should be taken to be a
hexadecimal number. For example, &F is 15 and &FF is 255. In
particular, it is important not to confuse &10 with ten (to find out
what it is type PRINT &10). The use of & may confuse many people
because $ is the most common symbol for hexadecimal but you soon
get used to it. To print a number in hex all you have to do is place ~
in front of it. For example, PRINT~255 produces FF. You can use
both & and ~ in combination with any of the indirection operators
to manipulate memory directly in hex. This is a very useful facility as
we shall see in this and later chapters.

BASIC's use of memory

The memory map given in Chapter One showed the general layout of the BBC Micro's address space in terms of ROM, RAM or I/O. However, when running BASIC, the available RAM has a fairly fixed use that can be seen in Figure 2.1. The top-most portion of RAM is always taken by high resolution graphics. The actual

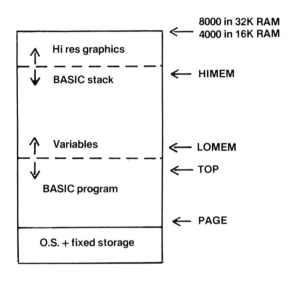

Fig. 2.1. RAM as used by BASIC.

amount that is used depends on the graphics mode selected (see Chapter Four) but the address of the first memory location below the area used for graphics is always available in the variable HIMEM. The bottom-most portion of memory is also used for something other than storing BASIC programs. It is used by the MOS (see the next chapter) to store details of how the machine is set up, i.e. what type of printer is in use etc., as storage for buffers such as the keyboard buffer and sound buffer etc., and as RAM storage for any programs in ROM. All-in-all, the lower area of memory is used for just about everything! An important area from the point of view of BASIC is &0400 to &0800 which is designated as the *language work area*. This is used by the BASIC ROM to store most but not all, of the information about a program as it is running. The area of memory from &0000 to &0100 is known as page zero and it is particularly useful because certain machine code instructions (see

Chapters Seven and Eight) only work with page zero. Thus, even though BASIC has a work area set aside for it, it does use some zero page locations. The actual amount of memory used by the MOS and other ROM programs varies according to what the machine configuration is. However, the address of the first free memory location can always be found in the variable PAGE. As a BASIC program is typed in or loaded from tape it is stored in memory starting at ?PAGE. The 'top' of the BASIC program – in fact the first free memory location after the BASIC program – can be found by using the function TOP. The variable LOMEM contains the address of the first memory location above the BASIC program that can be used to store variables that are created when the program is actually run. LOMEM usually contains the same address as TOP but you can change LOMEM to point to another area of memory if you want to (reasons why you might want to are suggested in Chapter Eight). The amount of memory that a BASIC program is using, not including any memory needed for variable storage, can be found by typing PRINT TOP-PAGE.

It is interesting to go through the changes in memory use that occur as a program is loaded and run. When the machine is first switched on all the memory pointers are set to their correct values. As a BASIC program is typed in or loaded, the value of TOP and LOMEM are adjusted so that they always point to the first free location above the program. When the program is RUN, memory is used starting from LOMEM to store variables as they are encountered within the program.

The area of memory just below HIMEM is also used for storage by a running BASIC program but only for temporary storage for things such as the return address for subroutines and procedures etc. Thus, as the program runs, memory is taken starting at LOMEM and extending upward – this is often referred to as the BASIC *heap* – and growing downward from HIMEM, which is often referred to as the BASIC *stack*. Obviously, if the running program changes the display mode then the value of HIMEM will change. If this were to happen when the BASIC stack was in use then it would crash the program; this is the reason why you can only change modes from the main program and not in a subroutine or procedure.

Now that we have a picture of how BASIC puts the RAM to work it is time to examine in detail how things are stored. First we will look at how the lines of a BASIC program are stored and then at how the different types of variables are stored.

The way BASIC is stored

Each line of BASIC that you type in has three parts – the line number, the keyword such as GOTO PRINT or REM, and the rest of the statement. This division also corresponds to the way that a line of BASIC is stored internally. The ASCII code for carriage return, i.e. &0D, marks the start of every line. Then follow two bytes that hold the line number in binary. The fourth memory location is used to store the length of the line. Finally, we reach the actual text of the BASIC statement. This is stored exactly as written in the form of ASCII code but with a few changes. For example, any keywords in the line are replaced by codes that can be stored in a single memory location. This makes good sense because it saves storage space and the code that is used is related to the ROM address of the machine code that implements the BASIC operation. (For a full list of key words see the User Guide.) This changing of keywords into codes is known as *tokenisation* and the codes are known as *tokens*.

You can see the format of the internal storage of a BASIC line in Figure 2.2. When there is no program in memory there is still a single

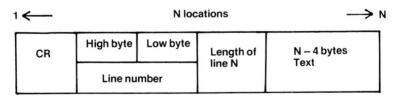

Fig. 2.2. Internal storage of a BASIC line.

carriage return stored so PAGE and TOP never point to exactly the same location. The end of a BASIC program is marked by a line number that has &F stored in the high byte of the line number. BBC BASIC line numbers must lie in the range 0 to &7FFF so using &FFxx as an end of program marker doesn't interfere with the normal numbering of a program. If you type NEW then all the BBC Micro does to delete the program is to write &FF in the high byte of the first line number and reset the pointers TOP and LOMEM. Because deleting a program with NEW doesn't alter anything else about the program, it is possible for OLD to restore the program by setting what was the high byte of the line number of the first line back to zero and then use the *length of line* information to scan through the memory to find the original end of the program and set the pointers TOP and LOMEM accordingly.

An interesting point is that neither LIST nor SAVE actually take any notice of TOP to find the end of a program. Instead they both use the end of program marker in the high byte of the line number to stop listing or saving a program. The sole purpose of TOP seems to be to govern where a new line of BASIC would be added to the program. It is also worth pointing out the amount of work that is involved in obeying a simple GOTO or GOSUB command. The program has to be searched for the line number used in the GOTO or GOSUB. This involves starting at the beginning of the program and comparing line numbers one at a time, using the length of line information to move on to the next line number until either the search is successful or the current line number is bigger than the one being searched for. This long-winded process is, of course, the reason why functions and procedures are faster than subroutines.

Handling variables – format and storage

There are two things of interest about the way BASIC handles variables. First, it would be interesting to know how to find out where any variable was stored. Secondly, it would then be useful to know the format used to store information in the different types of variable.

BBC BASIC uses a very clever method of keeping track of where it has placed a variable. When a program runs, each new variable that is encountered is allocated some space in the BASIC heap (starting at LOMEM). The address of the first free memory location in the heap is stored in &0002 and &0003 which, for want of a better name we will call 'freemem'. Thus, the storage of variables starts at LOMEM and goes up to freemem. New variables are allocated memory where freemem is pointing and then freemem is increased to point to the next free location. So far this is exactly what any other version of BASIC does to allocate storage to variables. What is special about BBC BASIC is the way that it keeps track of where each variable is.

Other versions of BASIC simply store the name of each variable as it occurs along with its value. When a variable is required a search is carried out of the entire BASIC heap. If you use a lot of variables this can take a long time! BBC BASIC, in an attempt to shorten the search time, keeps a separate list of variables for each letter of the alphabet, upper and lower case. In other words, if the first letter of a variable's name is A, it joins the 'capital A' list. If its first letter is a z, then it joins the lower case z list. When BBC BASIC wants to find a variable, it has only to search the list of variables that have the same first letter. As long as you don't start all your variables with the same letter this should be a quicker way of finding them.

The way that the separate lists are maintained is fairly simple. For each letter of the alphabet A–Z and a–z there is a start of list pointer which contains the address of the start of the list of variables that start with that letter. These pointers are stored in the language work-space area of memory from &0482 and &0483, which forms the pointer to all the variables starting with A, to &04F4 and &04F5, which points to the start of the list of variables beginning with z. To work out the address of the pointer to the list of all variables beginning with the letter stored in A\$, use (ASC(A\$)–65)*2+&0482 which gives the address of the least significant byte of the pointer. If there are no variables beginning with a particular letter then the corresponding pointer is set to zero. If there are variables beginning with a particular letter then the corresponding pointer contains the address of the first variable. The address of the second variable in the list is stored in the first two memory locations allocated to the first variable. Each variable in the list contains a pointer to the next variable in the list. The end of the list is marked by a zero address for the next variable.

The procedure for adding a variable to the BASIC heap is now a little more complicated than for the simple storage scheme described earlier but the increase in speed that results is well worth the trouble. To add a variable to the list you first have to find the end of the list by searching down its length until you find the first zero pointer. This may sound like a chore but of course it has to be done anyway to find out if the variable already exists! When the variable at the end of the list is found its pointer is changed to point to the same location as freemem. Then the space that the variable requires is allocated and freemem is changed to point once again to the first free memory location.

Now that we know how variables are allocated space and how to find where they are stored, the only thing left to discuss is the format used to store each type of variable. BBC BASIC recognises three fundamental or 'simple' data types – integer, real and string – and can handle arrays made up of any of the three types.

The storage format used for an integer variable can be seen in Figure 2.3. The first two locations form the pointer to the next variable with the same initial letter, as discussed above. These two bytes are zero if there is no next variable. The subsequent bytes are

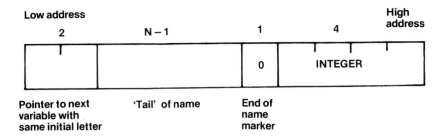

Low address · High address

2 · N − 1 · 1 · 4

0 · INTEGER

Pointer to next variable with same initial letter · 'Tail' of name · End of name marker

Fig. 2.3. Storage of an integer variable with N characters in its name (including the %).

used to record the rest of the variable's name minus the first letter but including the % sign to show that what follows is an integer. So, for example, a variable called TOTAL% would have its name stored as OTAL%. The end of the name is marked by a memory location with zero in it. Following this are four bytes that hold the actual integer value associated with the variable. The format that is used to store the value is 64-bit 2s complement. You can use the ! indirection operator to obtain its correct value.

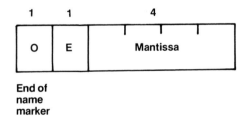

1 · 1 · 4

O · E · Mantissa

End of name marker

Fig. 2.4. Storage of a real variable.

Figure 2.4 shows the format used to store real variables. To be more precise, it shows only the part of the format that is different from the integer format. A real variable starts off with a pointer to the next variable and the rest of its name just like an integer variable but following the end of name marker are five bytes used to store a real value. A real value is stored in floating point form with a one byte exponent and four byte mantissa.

A string variable also starts off in the same way as an integer variable with a pointer to the next variable and the rest of the name including the $ sign. The rest of the string format consists of four bytes, as shown in Figure 2.5. The first two of these four bytes contain the address of the actual string of characters that are stored

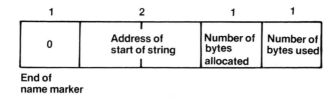

Fig. 2.5. Storage of a string variable.

in the string. The third byte is used to record the number of bytes allocated to the string for storing its value and the fourth byte records the number of bytes actually used (in other words, the length of the string). What is interesting about this format is that the string of characters that forms the string's value is stored away from the variable itself. This will be considered in more detail in the section on garbage collection.

Finally we come to the format used to store arrays. This initially follows that used for the same pattern as the simple variables but the name that is stored not only includes the $ or % sign but the (as well. The rest of its format can be seen in Figure 2.6. The first location following the end of name marker records the number of dimensions

1	1	2	2		
O	2*DIM + 1 L	No. of elements in first dimension	No. of elements in second dimension	. . . .	Variable elements

Fig. 2.6. Array storage.

in the array. To be precise, it is twice the number of dimensions plus one that is stored in this location which is the number of memory locations needed to store all of the other information about the array. Following this byte are pairs of memory locations, one pair for each dimension, recording the number of elements in each dimension. Following this information are the values that form the elements of the array.

Before leaving the subject of variable storage it is worth commenting on the way functions and procedures are handled. In the same way that variables are formed into lists so are functions and procedures. The memory locations &04F6 and &04F7 are used as a pointer to a list of procedures. Each item in the list has roughly the same format as a variable. The first pair of bytes point to the next procedure in the list, if any. Then comes the full name of the procedure ending with the usual zero byte. Following this are two bytes containing the address of the start of the procedure. The same technique is used to form a list of functions but in this case the initial pointer is formed by locations &04F8 and &04F9.

A heap dump program

To make the above information on variable storage etc. a little more concrete a variables, procedure and function dump program is given below. Not only does this serve to illustrate the points made above but it is a useful program in its own right.

```
9000 DEFPROCdump
9010 LOCAL X,Y
9020 FOR X=&0482 TO &04F4 STEP 2
9030 Y=?X+256*X?1
9040 IF Y<>0 THEN PROCvarlist(X,Y,0)
9050 NEXT X
9060 PRINT
9070 PROCother
9080 ENDPROC

9090 DEFPROCvarlist(X,Y,P)
9100 LOCAL A$,I,TYPE
9110 A$=STRING$(50,"X")
9120 A$=CHR$(65+(X-&0482)/2)
9130 TYPE=0
9140 PRINT TAB(0);^Y;TAB(5);
9150 I=2
9160 IF Y?I=0 THEN GOTO 9230
9170 A$=A$+CHR$(Y?I)
9180 IF Y?I=ASC("2") THEN TYPE=1
9190 IF Y?I=ASC("$") THEN TYPE=2
9200 IF Y?I=ASC("(") THEN TYPE=TYPE+100
9210 I=I+1
9220 GOTO 9160
9230 IF TYPE>99 THEN GOTO 9290
9240 IF P=1 THEN PRINT "PROC";A$;GOTO 9350
9250 IF P=2 THEN PRINT "FN";A$;GOTO 9350
9260 PRINT A$;TAB(10);TYPE;TAB(20);EVAL.(A$)
9270 IF TYPE=2 THEN PRINT TAB(20);Y?(I+3);
     TAB(30);Y?(I+4)
9280 GOTO 9350
9290 D=(Y?(I+1))-1
9300 PRINT A$;
9310 FOR Z=1 TO D STEP 2
9320 PRINT STR$(Y?(I+1+Z)+256*Y?(I+2+Z)-1);
     ",";
```

```
9330 NEXT Z
9340 PRINT CHR$(08);")"
9350 IF Y?1=0 THEN ENDPROC
9360 Y=?Y+256*Y?1
9370 GOTO 9120

9380 DEFPROCother
9390 LOCAL X,Y
9400 Y=?&04F6+256*?&04F7
9410 IF Y=0 THEN GOTO 9440
9420 X=0
9430 PROCvarlist(X,Y,1)
9440 Y=?&04F8+256*?&04F9
9450 IF Y=0 THEN ENDPROC
9460 X=0
9470 PROCvarlist(X,Y,2)
9480 ENDPROC
```

The first procedure, PROCdump, examines each of the variable pointers in turn and calls PROCvarlist if any variables are present in the list. Most of the work is done by PROCvarlist, which first puts together the full name of the variable – lines 9120 to 9220. While the full name of the variable is being constructed in A$, each character of the name is tested against %, $ and (to determine the TYPE of the variable. Once the full variable name is present in A$ the BASIC statement EVAL is used to print the contents of the variable by line 9260. If the variable was a string then line 9270 also prints the amount of storage allocated to the string and the amount of storage actually used. If the variable is an array then no attempt is made to print out its values; just its dimensions are printed. Line 9290 works out the number of dimensions in the array and lines 9310 to 9340 print the size of each dimension in turn. After all the details of the variable have been printed, lines 9350 to 9370 work out the address of the next variable with the same initial letter. If there is none, then control is returned to the dump procedure. After all the different variable lists have been processed, PROCother is called to print the active procedures and functions. PROCother simply checks the initial procedure and function list pointers and calls PROCvarlist to work out the names of each procedure or function in the list.

Notice that if you use PROCdump it will not only report any variables etc. employed by a main program with which it is being used in conjunction. It will also report all of its own variables, procedures and functions.

The resident integer variables

Although we have discussed the storage and format of the variables that can be used in BBC BASIC, we have ignored a set of very special and very useful variables – the resident integer variables. The names of the resident integer variables are @%A%,B%...Z%. Instead of being stored in the BASIC heap, these variables have a fixed area of the language work area set aside for them. As a result they exist whether you use them or not. They are not cleared or changed in any way by NEW, CLEAR or LOAD. In fact, apart from explicit assignment, the only thing that changes the value of a resident integer variable is switching the machine off and on again! It is often useful to know that the resident integer variables are stored starting with @% at &0400 with four bytes to each variable so that A%, for example, starts at &0404. The resident integer variables will be mentioned again in Chapters Seven and Eight.

Garbage collection

When a numeric variable is allocated space in the BASIC heap it is there to stay and it never needs to change the amount of storage allocated to it. However, string variables are very different and they can change their size all the way through the execution of a BASIC program. A string may start out holding only a few characters and then grow to the maximum size a string can be, i.e. 255 characters, and then shrink back to only a few characters again. As a string grows in size, more memory in the heap has to be allocated to it. When it grows smaller it would be efficient if the memory it released were returned to the heap, and this is usually referred to as *garbage collection*. However, garbage collection takes time and the BBC Micro is built for speed! When a string variable is first used, an entry in the format given in Figure 2.5 is created in the heap. The actual characters that make up the string are also stored in the heap and the address of the first character and its length are stored in the appropriate locations next to the string variable's name. In fact, a few more bytes than are necessary to store the string are allocated to allow the string to grow a bit before problems arise. If you reduce the length of the string then nothing happens apart from its current length being updated. In particular, the memory locations that are freed are not returned to the heap; instead, they are left ready for the string to increase in length again. If you add characters to the string to the point where all of its allocated space is used up, then to increase its length still more requires, obviously, some more memory to be allocated from the heap. This is not an easy matter because other variables and strings may be located just above the string in question. Allocating extra space, therefore, would mean moving everything above the string up in the memory. Considering the way that variables are linked together in separate lists, this would be no easy operation! Instead of this difficult move, the BBC Micro simply creates a new copy of the string's value at the top of the heap including some extra memory locations for future growth. If you think about this approach to creating more space for a string value you should be able to see that it is fast but very wasteful of memory. There can be a considerable number of *dead* copies of string values occupying valuable RAM storage because the BBC Micro fails to do any garbage collection.

To illustrate this problem consider the following short program:

```
10 A$=""
20 PROCSIZE
30 A$=A$+"A"
40 PRINT LEN(A$),;
50 GOTO 20

100 DEFPROCSIZE
110 PRINT ?2+256*?3-TOP
120 ENDPROC
```

The procedure PROCSIZE prints the current size of the BASIC heap by working out the difference between freemem and TOP. The program itself first sets up a string A$ that is initially set to the null string. Each time through the loop formed by lines 20 to 50 a single letter is added to the string and the size of the heap is printed. If you run this program you might be surprised how much storage it takes to hold 255 characters. The final line that the program prints indicates that the heap reaches nearly 4K bytes! The solution to this waste of storage is simple. If the string is defined to be the maximum size that it will ever be when it is first used no extra copies of it will ever be made. If you change line 10 of the above program to read:

```
10 A$=STRING$(255,"X"):A$=""
```

you will find that the final line of the program now reveals that it takes a much more reasonable 272 bytes to store a string 255 characters long. If you set strings equal to the maximum length that they are likely to reach during a program you will save a lot of memory! The way that strings are handled by the BBC Micro might seem a little crude but it really is the only way that it can be done and still achieve a fast BASIC.

LOCAL variables and the stack

Although we now know a lot about the way variables are stored we still do not know how local variables work. How can it be that a variable named in a LOCAL statement can replace any variable of the same name in the main program for the duration of the procedure or function in which it occurs and the original value stored in the variable still be intact at the end of the procedure? The answer to this question is surprisingly straightforward. When a function or a procedure is entered, any variables that are named in a LOCAL statement or that occur as parameters are searched for in the heap. If a variable with the same name is found then the value that is stored in it is stored on the BASIC stack. If the variable doesn't exist then it is created with an initial value of zero if it is numeric and the null string if it is a string. After the original value has been safely stored away on the stack, the variable can be used by the function or procedure without any worry about altering anything in the main program. The action is the same if the variable is a parameter except that after the value is stored on the stack the local variable is initialised to the value given to the parameter by the statement that referenced the function or procedure. Once the function or procedure has finished, the original values stored in any local variable are retrieved from the stack and are returned to their original places. Any local variable without counterparts of the same name are not destroyed; they are simply left set either to zero or the null string.

If you follow the way that the BASIC stack is used every time that a function or procedure is called, you should have no trouble in following how functions and procedures can be used recursively.

Conclusion

It would be possible to write an entire book on the subject of BBC BASIC! This chapter has dealt with some of its more interesting and immediately useful aspects. Much of the information it contains can be used to write programs that not only work faster and use less memory, but are also more logical and easier to debug.

Chapter Three
The Machine Operating System

The BBC Micro has so many unique features that it is difficult to pick out any one for special praise. Also it is easy to overlook its broader design philosophy because individual features capture the attention. The MOS (Machine Operating System) is a machine code program roughly 16K bytes in size. A program of this size rivals the BASIC in its complexity. However, unlike the BASIC ROM, it is difficult to sum up what the MOS actually does. It is responsible for so many different things that it would be easy to dismiss the MOS as simply a collection of all the 'odds and ends' that wouldn't fit into the BASIC ROM. However, this would be an underestimation of the careful thought that obviously went into writing the MOS. There are two approaches to building a machine. You can design the hardware and then implement a version of BASIC by interfacing it with the hardware directly. This can be thought of as the 'solve the problems as they arise' approach. For example, you would write things like printer drivers only when they were required by a BASIC statement that listed a program to a printer. Writing a version of BASIC with this sort of approach tends to take short cuts to providing access to hardware features which results in a shorter BASIC interpreter. However, it also tends to transmit any difficulties and shortcomings in the hardware back to the programmer. The second approach to building a machine starts in the same way with the design of the hardware, but before implementing BASIC an extra *layer* of software is *installed* to iron out any problems and generally improve the hardware's appearance. In the BBC Micro this extra layer of software is provided in the MOS. In some senses it is more accurate to think of the BBC Micro, its hardware and the MOS providing an environment that is suitable for running BASIC or any other high level language. Another way of looking at this is that the MOS creates a 'soft machine' that is easier to use and more sophisticated than the underlying 'hard machine'. So although the

MOS has to do a very wide range of things, it has a single purpose.

The rest of this chapter looks at some of the interesting things that you can do with the MOS. Even though the MOS has a single purpose it is impossible to find a logical order in which to discuss it because of the wide range of things that it does to achieve this purpose. There has already been a number of versions of the MOS issued since the BBC Micro was first produced. The version described in this book is Version 1. This is the first version of the MOS to include all of the intended features. To find out which version you have simply type *FX 0. If you have an earlier version and find that you lack facilities that you wish to use, then contact your dealer for a new ROM.

In general, it is true to say that the MOS provides software to handle the following I/O devices:

- The graphics display and VDU drivers.
- Printer and serial I/O.
- Cassette filing system.
- Keyboard.
- A to D convertor.
- Sound generator.
- The tube.

It also makes extensive use of interrupts to improve the overall performance of the machine.

There are three ways that the MOS is used by the programmer. First, many BASIC commands are implemented directly by the MOS. Secondly, there is a range of MOS commands such as *FX and *KEY which cause the MOS to carry out certain tasks. Finally, there are machine code routines within the MOS that the assembly language programmer can use. It is difficult to avoid considering the use of the MOS from assembly language programs here even though assembly language is not discussed until Chapter Seven. The MOS is useful to a BASIC programmer but it is fascinating from the point of view of assembly language! Any sections that make reference to assembly language should be read without worrying too much about understanding the material completely. You will only find this chapter completely comprehensible after you have made the acquaintance of assembly language in Chapters Seven and Eight. If you have no desire to learn assembly language then don't worry – there is still much to be gained by using the MOS from BASIC.

Indirection and MOS subroutines

One important feature of the MOS is that all its important subroutines are available for use by the assembly language programmer. In addition, the assembly language programmer can actually replace any of the important subroutines by user-defined routines. The way that this works is particularly simple. All external MOS subroutines are used by a CALL to the region &FF00 to &FFFF. For example, the 'print a character on the screen' subroutine, OSWRCH, is positioned at &FFEE. However, at this high memory location there is very little of the code for each of the subroutines. In fact, all that happens is a jump to the true location of the subroutine inside the main part of the MOS ROM. The address of the true location of the subroutine is obtained from RAM in the region &200–&2FF which is known as the *indirection* area. For example, the true address of the OSWRCH subroutine is contained in &20F. You can find a table of MOS subroutines, their fixed addresses and their indirection routines on page 452 of the User Guide. The advantage of this roundabout method of getting to the MOS subroutines is two-fold. First, the true locations of the MOS subroutines can be changed in later versions without invalidating user programs. Secondly, by changing the address stored in the indirection area of RAM the user can intercept MOS calls and supply alternative versions.

The MOS subroutines that are available to the user fall into three categories – tape I/O routines, screen and keyboard I/O routines and three miscellaneous routines. The tape I/O routines OSFIND, OSGBPB, OSBPUT, OSARGS and OSFILE are used by BASIC to manipulate cassette files and may be used by the assembly language programmer for the same purpose. They are all adequately described in the User Guide and it is unlikely that a programmer would ever want to replace them with special versions.

The keyboard and screen I/O routines are OSRDCH, OSASCI, OSNEWL and OSWRCH. These form the basic way of handling text from BASIC and assembly language programs. Once again, they are well described in the User Guide and no further comment is necessary.

The three miscellaneous subroutines are quite another matter, however! Between them they carry out so many different functions that it is worth highlighting some of the possible ways that they could be used. The three subroutines are OSBYTE, OSWORD and OSCLI. OSBYTE and OSWORD are general purpose subroutines that can be used to configure the BBC Micro or control I/O devices. The OSCLI subroutine is a command line interpreter that allows the BASIC programmer direct access to the OSBYTE subroutine. Any command line that starts with an asterisk, such as *MOTOR 1, is not processed by the BASIC interpreter; instead it is passed to the OSCLI subroutine for processing. The OSCLI decodes the command and then calls the OSBYTE subroutine to carry out the correct action. Most of operating system commands are of the form *FX 'parameters' but some are used so often that they are given names all of their own, for example, *MOTOR, *TAPE etc. Thus, OSBYTE calls that do not need to return any results are available to the BASIC programmer as operating system commands. The OSBYTE calls that return results can only be used from BASIC via the USR function. The OSBYTE subroutine deals with everything that can be specified using only three bytes (these are held in the A,X and Y registers). Anything that needs more than three bytes is handled by the OSWORD subroutine. As there is no simple way of passing more than three bytes to an assembly language subroutine, OSWORD calls can really only be used by assembly language programs.

Although the User Guide describes all the OSBYTE and OSWORD calls in some detail it doesn't always make clear what they might be used for. In order to avoid repeating the details given in the User Guide, a complete list of calls will not be given here. Instead, the sort of thing that the less obvious calls might be used for will be briefly described.

The first *FX call that is worthy of further discussion is *FX 4. Following *FX 4,1 the five cursor keys return ASCII codes just like the other keys on the keyboard. The normal condition is for the cursor keys not to return ASCII codes but move the cursor round the screen. This condition can be restored by *FX 4,0. There are two reasons why you might want the cursor keys to return ASCII codes. First, you may simply want to disable the cursor editing facility in an applications program to stop inexperienced users from getting out of their depth. Secondly, if you want to use the four *arrow* keys to control the movement of a graphics character in a game, then the only way that this can be done is for the cursor keys to return ASCII codes.

The *FX 11 call sets the time that a key has to be held down before it starts to auto repeat. The required time delay in centi-seconds is the only parameter in the call, and if you specify a time of zero then the auto repeat is disabled. *FX 12 sets the rate at which keys auto repeat. Once again there is a single parameter that sets the time between repeats in centi-seconds. These two calls are often used together to change the response of the keyboard. For example, it is a good idea to turn the auto repeat facility off in applications programs. However, in games programs where a quick response is required, the keyboard can be set to auto repeat after only 1 centi-second and produce characters at the same rate. By using *FX 11 and *FX 12, the BBC Micro's keyboard's response can be adjusted to suit any situation.

One *FX call that seems particularly puzzling is *FX 138 which inserts a character into the keyboard buffer. The format of the call is *FX 138,0 'ASCII code' which inserts the character whose code is 'ASCII code' into the keyboard buffer. Any characters placed in the keyboard buffer in this way are treated in exactly the same way as if they had been typed in. The BBC Micro doesn't care where the characters in the keyboard buffer come from, only what they are. This means that a running program can place a string of characters in the keyboard buffer and when the program ends the string will be obeyed as if it had been typed in. For example, if the string 'LIST' followed by a carriage return is placed in the keyboard buffer by a running program, then the program effectively lists itself as soon as it stops! To see this in action try:

```
10 *FX 138,0,76
20 *FX 138,0,73
30 *FX 138,0,83
40 *FX 138,0,84
50 *FX 138,0,13
```

This ability for a running program to 'type on the keyboard' is something to be kept in mind when all else fails. It can be used to good advantage to provide default answers to questions asked by an applications program. For example, if you remove line 50 from the above program, the keyboard buffer is filled with LIST but without the carriage return. If you also add 60 INPUT A$ to the end of the program you will see that the word LIST appears after the usual '?' prompt printed by the INPUT statement. To accept it, all you have to do is press RETURN; to reject it you backspace and type whatever you want.

The final *FX code that deserves special mention is *FX 229. The call *FX 229,1 disables the action of the ESCAPE key and makes it return the ASCII code 27. In other words, following *FX 229,1 the ESCAPE key no longer interrupts the running of a BASIC program. To restore its normal action use *FX 229,0. Using this call

and the definition of *KEY 10 as OLD I MRUN I M makes a BASIC
program completely unstoppable. The call disables the ESCAPE
key and the definition of key 10 (the BREAK key) effectively
disables the BREAK key. The only way to stop the program is to
switch the machine off.

Adding commands

The OSCLI subroutine provides a simple method of adding new
commands to the MOS or to BASIC. Any line that starts with an
asterisk, be it a direct command or in a BASIC program, is handled
by the OSCLI subroutine at &FFF7. As mentioned earlier, all the
MOS subroutines indirect through RAM locations and OSCLI is
no exception. The address of the actual OSCLI subroutine is stored
in &0208 and &0209. To add new commands, we could intercept the
OSCLI call by changing the address stored in &0208 to point to a
specially written assembly language routine. Although assembly
language isn't discussed until Chapter Seven, it is worth including an
example here.
    Consider the following short program:

```
10 DIM CODE% 10
20 ?&208=CODE% AND &00FF
30 ?&209=(CODE% AND &FF00)/&FF
40 P%=CODE%
50 [ LDA #65
60   JSR &FFEE
70   RTS
80 ]
90 FOR I=1 TO 10
100 *
110 NEXT I
```

Lines 40 to 70 form an assembly language program that simply
prints the letter A on the screen. Lines 20 and 30 change the address
of OSCLI to the address of the 'print letter A' routine. Lines 80 to
100 form a perfectly simple FOR loop apart from the fact that line 90
is nothing but an asterisk! If you run the program you will find that
the letter A is printed on the screen ten times, thus proving that the
asterisk now means 'print the letter A'.
    In any real application, the address of the OSCLI subroutine
would be saved within the new assembly language routine. The new
routine would check to see that what followed the asterisk was a
command that was its concern. For example, we might decide to call

the 'print A' routine by the command *PRINTA and the first job that the routine would do would be to check that the word 'PRINTA' followed the asterisk. If this was not the case then the OSCLI proper would be called using the address that was originally stored in the RAM locations. In this way new commands can be added to the existing set of commands rather than replacing them.

The video display

The hardware and software that makes up the video display is discussed fully in the next chapter. However, it is worth pointing out that the MOS is entirely responsible for the software that drives the video hardware. In particular, the MOS contains the VDU drivers and the character generator table. The method of communication with the video section of the MOS is not via a long list of subroutine calls. Instead, the OSWRCH subroutine detects and acts upon an extended set of ASCII control codes. These control codes are sent to the OSWRCH subroutine in exactly the same way as a printable character, but their effects can be very extensive. In BASIC the command VDU appears to be the fundamental graphics command. In fact, all it does is to transmit the necessary control codes to the VDU drivers via the OSWRCH subroutine. So the following are equivalent:

```
VDU 8

PRINT CHR$(08);

[ LDA #8
  JSR &FFEE
]
```

and each sends a backspace command to the VDU drivers. In practice, many of the control codes are followed by a number of parameters.

Interrupts

The BBC Micro makes extensive use of interrupts to improve its overall performance. An interrupt is simply a way of switching the 'attention' of the 6502 processor inside the machine from one task to another and back again. For example, if a BASIC program is running, then the 6502 is giving its full attention to this task. If, however, a key is pressed on the keyboard this causes an interrupt which makes the 6502 stop what it is doing and start running the keyboard service routine in the MOS. This finds out which key was pressed and stores the correct ASCII value in the keyboard buffer. Once the keyboard is dealt with, the 6502 returns to the original task of running your BASIC program, starting from the point where it was interrupted. This idea is not a difficult one – after all, humans respond to interrupts. If you are reading a book and the telephone rings then you process this interrupt by marking your place in the book, answering the telephone and then returning to your reading at the point where you were interrupted. However, even though the idea of an interrupt is simple in theory, in practice things are often difficult to handle. The trouble is that an interrupt may happen at any time and may be caused by any number of devices. For example, as well as the keyboard interrupt the 6502 has to service an interrupt from a timer in VIA–A every one hundredth of a second. On receiving this timer interrupt, all the 6502 does is to increment the value stored in the variable TIME but how does it know where the interrupt came from? Was it from the keyboard or was it from the timer? In fact, there are many sources of interrupts that we haven't yet considered. The key to finding out which device has caused an interrupt is contained in the hardware causing the interrupt. Each I/O device that can cause an interrupt has an a bit known as an interrupt flag somewhere in its status register. This flag is normally set to zero but if the device has caused an interrupt then it is set to one. The method of finding which device has caused an interrupt is simply to examine each of the I/O devices' interrupt flags to find which are set to one.

As already mentioned, the BBC Micro makes extensive use of interrupts. However, if you do not intend to become involved with writing assembly language programs that make use of interrupts then you can ignore this fact. The only unexpected consequence it has is that you cannot use delay loops for exact timing simply because you cannot always guarantee that the 6502 is executing your program – it might be off servicing an interrupt for some part of the time! Apart from this, interrupts simply alter the general way that the BBC Micro behaves. For example, the fact that the keyboard is serviced by an interrupt as described in the last paragraph means that anything that you type on the keyboard goes into the keyboard buffer even if the computer appears to be busy doing something else – i.e. it provides type-ahead. The overall effect of interrupts on the

BBC Micro is to give it the appearance of being able to do more than one thing at a time!

If you are interested in making use of interrupts in assembly language programs, then you will certainly need to know a little more than outlined above. The 6502 recognises three distinct types of interrupt – NMI or Non-Maskable Interrupts, IRQ or Interrupt ReQuest and BRK or Break. The first type, NMI, is strictly reserved for use by the disc operating system and need not concern us further. All the other I/O devices that can cause interrupts use the IRQ interrupt. The BRK interrupt is a little different in that it is a software interrupt. A software interrupt is exactly the same as a normal interrupt except for the fact that it originates internally rather than being caused by an external device. In fact, 6502 assembly language includes the mnemonic BRK which causes a BRK interrupt to occur.

When the machine detects an IRQ interrupt it immediately passes control to a routine whose address is stored in &0204 (IRQV1). In other words, it indirects through this location in the same way as the MOS subroutines indirect through their own particular locations. The standard MOS routine to handle interrupts looks at the interrupt flags of all the devices that it knows about to discover the source of the interrupt. If it finds it then the appropriate action is carried out. For example, if it finds that the timer is responsible for the interrupt it will increment TIME and then return control to the program that was interrupted. However, it is possible that some I/O device that the MOS doesn't know anything about has caused the interrupt. In this case the standard interrupt service routine will not locate the cause of the interrupt. When this happens, control is passed to the routine whose address is stored in &0206 (IRQV2). Of course, this routine has to be supplied by the user to handle the interrupt in the appropriate way. When the user interrupt handler has finished it should return control to the MOS interrupt handler (by RTS) which will finish the interrupt procedure and return control to the program that was interrupted. Thus, adding routines is fairly straightforward. If you cannot afford to wait while the MOS checks all its possible sources of interrupts then you could intercept the IRQ interrupt at IRQV1 instead of IRQV2. In this case, of course, you should check, and possibly deal with, your source of interrupts and then pass control to the MOS interrupt service routine (whose address was originally in IRQV1).

The BRK interrupt is used by BASIC to report errors. How this is done is well-described in the User Guide and so will not be repeated here. As BRK indirects through &0202, it, too can be intercepted and handled by a user-supplied routine as required.

Interrupts that the MOS can handle might still be of interest to the user. For example, it may be that a user program needs to know when any key has been pressed although it is quite happy for the MOS to handle the interrupt. To deal with this requirement the MOS recognises a number of *events*. An event is either an interrupt or something that is detected during an interrupt that the MOS can handle perfectly well on its own. However, the MOS will inform the user of the event's occurrence on request. The normal state of affairs is for all events to be disabled. If an enabled event occurs, however, then control is passed to the routine whose address is stored in &0220. The events are enabled using *FX 14, 'code' where 'code' is one of the following:

Code	Event	
0	A buffer is empty	X=buffer identity
1	A buffer is full	X=buffer identity
		Y=character that couldn't be stored
2	A key has been pressed	
3	ADC conversion complete	
4	Start of TV field pulse	
5	Interval timer crossing zero	
6	Escape condition detected	

To disable an event, the same codes should be used in *FX 13,code. Notice that any normal interrupt handling happens before an enabled event indirects through &0220.

As a demonstration of how events work, type in and run the following program:

```
10 DIM CODE% 20
20 ?&220=CODE% AND &00FF
30 ?&221=(CODE% AND &FF00)/&FF
40 P%=CODE%
50 [ LDA #65
60   JSR &FFEE
70   RTS
80 ]
```

You might recognise the 'print an A' assembly language subroutine, that has been used in earlier examples, in lines 50 to 80. However, in this case its address is placed in &0220 and &0221. This means that following this program, any enabled event will cause a letter A to be printed on the screen every time it happens. To see this in action simply use *FX 14,code to enable the event of your choice. For example, following *FX 14,2 you will see a letter A printed following every character you type on the keyboard! Following *FX 14,4 you will see the letter A appear on the screen almost continuously – a field pulse event occurs every fiftieth of a second! To recover from most of the above examples it is easier to press BREAK and then type OLD and run the program again rather than try to disable the event with *FX 13,code – the A's appearing on the screen make typing difficult! Although this is not a very useful example, it does show how events can be used. A typical real example would be to synchronise the running of a program to the start of a TV frame display. Dealing with characters typed on the keyboard as soon as they are typed is another practical example.

Conclusion

The MOS is a very complex piece of software. Many of its functions are concerned with important I/O devices such as the graphics display, the sound generator and the A to D convertor, and these are discussed in the next three chapters. In this chapter, some of the less obvious features of the MOS have been described so that the BASIC programmer and assembly language programmer can both begin to make good use of the range of facilities available. It should also have made apparent just how clever the BBC Micro's MOS is.

Chapter Four
The Video Display

A large part of the BBC Micro's hardware and software is concerned with producing an excellent and extremely versatile video display. Indeed it is so good that many people are buying BBC Micros to use as colour video terminals to other computers! In this chapter we will examine both the hardware and the software aspects of the video display.

As with all practical arrangements of hardware and software there is a price to be paid for every advantage gained. In the case of the video display the biggest disadvantage is the large amount of memory used for the high resolution screens. As much as 20K of RAM can be used by the video display leaving only 16K of RAM for user programs and system use. As the system can use 3–4K, an applications program can find itself left with as little as 12K of RAM. Because of this need for large amounts of memory, not all modes are available on a Model A machine. If you have a Model A machine then upgrade as soon as you can because you are missing a lot! In the rest of this chapter all modes of the video display will be discussed, including those present only on the Model B.

Not all of the display modes take so much memory. Mode 7 teletext graphics take a remarkably small 1K and can produce some very good graphics in eight colours. However, the way mode 7 works is distinctly different from all the other modes so it is given a section at the end of the chapter all to itself. Whatever mode you are using there is no doubt that the best quality display is produced by a colour monitor driven by the RGB connector. However, you can still use the highest resolution graphics on a standard colour TV set. The BBC Micro working in black and white is useful but not nearly so much fun!

The video hardware

A brief description of the video hardware was given in Chapter One but without really explaining the way that the video information was stored in memory. The BBC Micro, like many others, uses memory-mapped graphics but it uses it in a way that is very different. Most machines that generate their own video output set aside an area of memory where the ASCII (or similar) codes of the characters to be displayed are stored. As each character's code can fit into eight bits, one memory location is used for every possible display position on the screen. For example, if you have a screen of 40 characters by 20 lines then you need 40 times 20 (i.e. 800) memory locations. The way in which these memory locations are made to correspond to positions on the screen varies from machine to machine. One possible arrangement is that the first memory location corresponds to the character displayed in the top left-hand corner of the screen, subsequent memory locations corresponding to screen locations to the left of the first until the end of the line is reached, with a new line starting at the far left-hand side again (see Figure 4.1). The way that the memory is associated with the different display positions on the screen is known as the *screen memory map*. Obviously, if you know the screen memory map for a particular machine then you can write

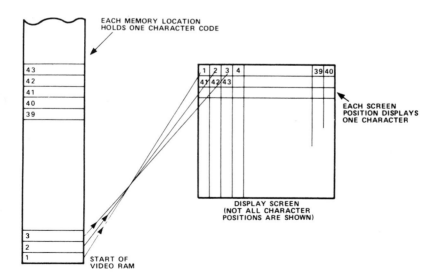

Fig. 4.1. The screen memory map for a 40 column screen. (Reprinted by permission of *Computing Today.*)

programs that can change the screen display by going straight to the correct memory location instead of using a PRINT or PLOT statement. This can be the quickest and sometimes simplest way of changing the screen and is often the only way of producing good moving graphics.

As mentioned earlier, the BBC Micro, in all but mode 7, uses a very different method of producing a memory-mapped screen. Instead of storing the ASCII code of the character to be displayed, the BBC Micro stores a bit pattern corresponding to the *shape* of the character. To make this clear it is worth considering the way other micros convert the ASCII code stored at each memory location into a character displayed on the screen.

A TV picture is built up from a series of lines and each row of characters takes a number of lines. Each character is formed from a number of dots which may be turned on or off. In this respect, the BBC Micro is no different from the rest and uses eight lines of eight dots for each character (see Figure 4.2). However, other micros produce this pattern of dots on the screen by using an extra chunk of

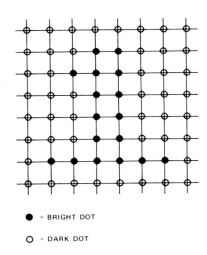

● = BRIGHT DOT

○ = DARK DOT

Fig. 4.2. An eight by eight dot matrix showing the character '1'. (Reprinted by permission of *Computing Today.*)

memory that is accessible only to the video display electronics. This extra chunk of memory is normally called a *character generator* but it is nothing more than a ROM containing the information about which dots should be off, and which on, to form the image of a particular character. It is because this ROM memory is available only to the display electronics that it is normally not counted as part of the computer's memory. If you want to know how much memory is involved in a character generator all you have to do is multiply the total number of dots used to make up a character by the total number of possible characters and divide by eight. This is because the ROM has to store the dot pattern of every character that can be displayed and each dot requires one bit. For the 8 by 8 array of dots used by the BBC Micro, a ROM to generate the character set would have to be 2K bytes in size. The usual method of displaying characters on a screen using a character generator is simply to use the ASCII code stored in the computer's memory as an address to select the location in the ROM that stores the dot pattern for that character (see Figure 4.3). Instead of using this *classical* approach to video display, the

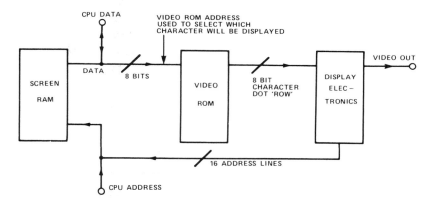

Fig. 4.3. A 'classical' video circuit design. (Reprinted by permission of *Computing Today*.)

BBC Micro (except in mode 7) dispenses with a character generator ROM and stores the dot pattern of the character to be displayed in RAM. The disadvantage of this method is that each screen location needs enough RAM to store all the dots for a single character – in the case of the BBC Micro this amounts to eight bytes per screen location. This means that in mode 4, for example, with 32 lines of 40 characters the total RAM required is 32 times 40 times 8 i.e. 10K bytes, and all this RAM is taken from the user RAM that you use to store programs and data. In other words, for a given screen size, the BBC Micro uses eight times the amount of screen RAM that the classical display method would require. This is because it stores the entire dot pattern for each character where the classical method stores an eight-bit code instead. The method that the BBC Micro uses is often called a *bit-mapped display* because every bit in the screen RAM corresponds to a dot on the video screen. We can still ask for the screen memory map in this case but now it will tell us how dots on the screen correspond to bits in memory locations rather than how whole characters correspond to codes stored in memory locations.

Given the extra memory that the BBC Micro has to use to produce its display, you might be wondering what the advantages are. The main advantage is that you can produce high resolution graphics and text characters using the same hardware. Every dot on the screen corresponds to a bit in the memory location so instead of storing the dot pattern corresponding to a character, you can change individual bits in the memory to produce lines and other shapes. Also, because the same basic method is used to display characters and to produce high resolution graphics you can mix both anywhere on the screen. A second advantage is that the character set is not restricted to whatever is stored in the character generator ROM and you can therefore define new characters. These two advantages give the BBC Micro a freedom in handling both graphics and characters that is difficult to match using any other method. For comparison, the Apple uses a bit-mapped display for its high resolution graphics but uses a standard character generator for its text modes and so has difficulties in freely mixing text and graphics without extra software (shape tables). On the other hand, the PET uses a character generator for both text and graphics and so can mix them freely but the range of graphics is limited to the *graphics characters* already defined in its ROM.

Colour

The above discussion of the BBC video generator ignores the fact that each dot displayed on the screen can be any of up to sixteen colours. So far we have assumed that each bit in the video memory produces a dot on the screen. This is true in a two-colour mode such as mode 4. As each bit can be either a zero or a one, its value can select one of two colours. The colour produced by a zero bit is called the *background colour* and the one produced by a one is known as the *foreground colour*. The reason for this is that the shapes on the screen are normally formed by patterns of ones against a background of zeros. However, if you select a four- or sixteen-colour mode then one bit per dot on the screen is clearly not enough. To select one of four colours you need two bits, and to select one of sixteen colours you need four bits. Thus, in a four-colour mode (modes 1 and 5) the value of two bits in the video memory determine the colour of one dot on the screen. In the only sixteen-colour mode, mode 2, it takes the values of four bits stored in video memory to determine the colour of one dot on the screen. As a memory location can hold eight bits, a single memory location can hold the colour values of eight dots in a two-colour mode, four dots in a four-colour mode and two dots in a sixteen-colour mode. How to find the bits that correspond to a single dot is discussed in the next section on memory maps but you should now be able to see why each display mode takes the amount of memory that it does.

The screen memory map for mode 4

What the use of a bit-mapped display means for the programmer is that, unlike machines such as the PET where storing a byte in a memory location causes a complete character to appear on the screen, storing a byte in the BBC Micro's display memory causes a pattern of dots on a single line to appear. All that we need to know now is how each memory location corresponds to a screen position – in other words, the screen memory map for each mode.

For simplicity it is better to start by considering a two-colour mode such as mode 4. The best way to discover the memory map for mode 4 is via a small test program. If we start at the lowest screen address and store a byte consisting of all ones then a short line of dots will appear somewhere on the screen. If the BBC Micro uses a fairly normal screen memory map, the line should appear in either the top left or bottom right corner. If you run the following program:

```
10 MODE 4
20 ?HIMEM=&FF
30 STOP
```

then you should see a short horizontal line in the top far left-hand corner. If you don't then it's possible that it's just off the part of the screen that your TV displays and a slight adjustment of the controls should make the line visible. If this fails then try *TV 254. This will move the whole display down by two lines. The program works by first selecting mode 4 and then (in line 20) storing the hex value FF in the memory location whose address is stored in HIMEM. The variable HIMEM stores the address of the first screen location in any mode, and FF in binary is eight ones and so produces a row of eight dots. We now know that the first (lowest) screen address corresponds to the top left-hand corner.

To find out how the rest of the screen memory map is arranged try the following program:

```
10 MODE 4
20 FOR I=0 TO 7
30 ?(HIMEM+I)=&FF
40 NEXT I
50 GOTO 50
```

This stores the hex value FF in eight consecutive memory locations. What is surprising about the result of this program is that, instead of producing a thin line eight characters long across the top of the screen, it displays a solid block about the same size as a normal character. The screen memory map for the BBC Micro is such that the first eight memory locations form the dot matrix for the first character. The next eight form the dot matrix for the character to the right of the first and so on to the end of a line. To see the screen memory map in action try the following:

```
10 MODE 4
20 I=0
30 ?(HIMEM+I)=&FF
40 I=I+1
50 FOR J=1 TO 50
60 NEXT J
70 GOTO 30
```

You should see the screen fill up, character position by character position. You can use this program to explore the possibilities of storing graphics data directly into the screen. In most other versions of BASIC, access to memory locations is via the command POKE, which stores values in memory locations, and the function PEEK, which returns the value stored in a memory location. For this reason storing data directly to screen location is usually called POKEing the screen and, similarly, finding out what is stored in a screen location is usually called PEEKing the screen. To see that things other than solid lines can be POKEd to the screen try altering line 30 to:

```
30 ?(HIMEM+I)=RND(255)
```

and removing the delay loop formed by 50 and 60.

Using the information obtained from the above programs, we can work out a simple equation that will give the address of any screen location:

```
address=HIMEM+(X+Y*40)*8+N
```

which gives the address of the Nth line making up the character at the screen location X,Y. (N,X and Y all start from zero in the top left-hand corner.)

The screen memory map – for other modes

The memory map for any two-colour mode is easy to deduce from that of mode 4. For example, mode 3 has eighty characters to a line and 25 lines so the address of any screen location is given by:

```
address=HIMEM+(X+Y*80)*8+N
```

The corresponding expression for mode 6 with 40 characters on each of 25 lines is:

```
address=HIMEM+(X+Y*40)*8+N
```

Finally, that for mode 0 with 80 characters and 32 lines is:

```
address=HIMEM+(X+Y*80)*8+N
```

Notice that the only thing that affects the expression is the number of characters to a line. The number of lines on the screen affects the largest value of Y that can be used, of course. Modes 3 and 6 are different from the other two-colour mode in that they are text only displays. The only reason that they cannot handle graphics is that there is *dead* space between each line of text that cannot be affected in any way. In mode 4 a full 32 lines of character locations fill the screen completely. However, there are only 25 lines of character locations in modes 3 and 6 and these are also spread out to fill the screen. This is done by leaving a little space between each line and this is the origin of the dead space seen in each of these modes. To see this dead space try the following program:

```
10 MODE 6
20 VDU 19,0,4,0,0,0
```

The way that VDU 19 works will be discussed later but meanwhile notice that line 20 sets the background colour to blue. The dead space then shows clearly as black lines.

The complication that arises with four- and sixteen-colour modes is due to the need for more than one bit to represent each dot on the screen. How are the extra bits organised in the memory map of the other modes? The answer to this question is that the fundamental memory map outlined for mode 4 is used for all the other modes except of course that each point on the screen is now determined by a small group of bits in each memory location. For example, in mode 4 a memory location holding eight bits gives rise to eight dots but in mode 5 (a four-colour mode) the same memory location only gives rise to *four* dots. In this case each group of two bits determines which of the four colours a point will be (see Figure 4.4).

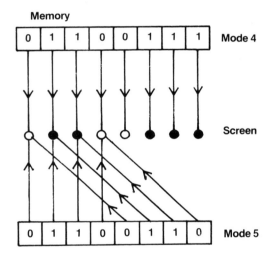

Fig. 4.4. The correspondence between memory and screen for Mode 4 and Mode 5.

The best way to investigate the memory maps of the other graphics modes is to use the programs given in the last section but change line 10 to give the required mode. In mode 5, as each block of eight memory locations now corresponds to only eight rows of four dots and each character still needs eight rows of eight dots to be displayed, it should be obvious that the storage of a single character involves two such blocks – one for the left-hand side and one for the right-hand side. Thus, the expression for the memory location corresponding to a row of dots in mode 5 (with 20 characters to a line) is:

```
address=HIMEM+(R+2*X+Y*20)*8+N
```

and in mode 1 (with 40 characters to a line):

```
address=HIMEM+(R+2*X+Y*40)*8+N
```

where X and Y are the column and line numbers of the character location, N is the number of the row of dots making up the character and R is set to 1 if it is in the right half of the character and to zero otherwise.

In the sixteen-colour mode 2 each memory location produces only two dots but the same overall pattern is maintained. Each set of eight memory locations produces a block two dots wide by eight high. Once again, a character needs an eight by eight block of dots so four of these smaller blocks are used to produce each character. If we number these smaller blocks as 0 to 3 starting at the left then the address of the memory location holding the Nth row of block B at character location X,Y is given by:

```
address=HIMEM+(4*X+B+Y*20)*8+N
```

The only question still left unanswered concerns the organisation of the bits within each memory location. In a two-colour mode, the contents of each memory location produces a row of eight dots, with the most significant bit corresponding to the left-most bit on the screen. This can be seen in Figure 4.5. In a four-colour mode the

M.S.B. bit 7	6	5	4	3	2	1	L.S.B. 0	
1	2	3	4	5	6	7	8	Dot number

Fig. 4.5. Bits to dots in a two-colour mode.

contents of a memory location control the colour of a row of four dots. The way that the bits pair to produce this row of four dots can be seen in Figure 4.6. (Notice that this is not the most obvious way to pair bits in a memory location.) Finally, the way that the eight bits in each memory location group to control the colour of two dots in a sixteen-colour mode can be seen in Figure 4.7.

All this may seem a little complicated. Compared to the way other computers work it is, but if you want to have the sort of freedom of

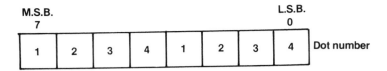

Fig. 4.6. Bits to dots in a four-colour mode.

action that the BBC Micro allows there is no other way of doing it! In practice, the use of direct memory-mapped graphics is limited to either mode 4 where it is easy, or involving assembler where everything is more difficult! Seriously though, POKEing the screen is something that is not as useful on the BBC Micro as on other machines – partly because it is more difficult except in two-colour modes and partly because the BASIC provides all sorts of features that make it unnecessary. What is more important is that a knowledge of the screen memory map allows you to find out quickly what is stored at any screen location.

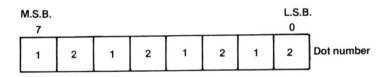

Fig. 4.7. Bits to dots in a sixteen-colour mode.

PEEKing the screen

This brings us to the topic of PEEKing the screen to see what character is stored at a particular location. This is easy in machines such as the PET – all you have to do is to PEEK the screen location and this returns the ASCII code of the character stored at that position. For the BBC Micro things are not quite as easy. The first problem is that PEEKing a screen location in a two-colour mode returns the dot pattern of a row of the characters stored at the location. This is not as useful as the ASCII code because, in general, it is not enough to identify the character – for example, it is possible for two characters to have the same dot pattern in every row except one! The second problem is that for the modes that use more than two colours, even a single row of dots from a character is difficult to obtain without a number of PEEKs and quite a bit of logic.

This might make you think that screen PEEKs are not worth the trouble on the BBC machine. However, for mode 4 things are easier than they look. The general problem of deciding what character is stored at a screen location is difficult even in mode 4 but in most graphics-based applications this is more than we want to do. Instead of identifying what character from the set of all possible characters is present, it is usually enough to decide which of two or three characters is there. For example, if you are using 'O' to represent one type of player and 'X' to represent another then you only have to discover if the character stored at a location is one of blank, O or X. This is a much easier problem as it should be possible to find a row of dots that is different in each character. If this *is* possible then you can tell the three characters apart by PEEKing that one row! In the case of blank, X and O, any row will distinguish them. For example, row three corresponds to 0, 24 and 102 respectively. As we know the screen memory map for mode 4, we can write a function that will return the address of a particular row of a screen location:

```
100 DEF FNS(X,Y,N)=HIMEM+(X+40*Y)*8+N
```

FNS will return the address of the screen location corresponding to the character position X,Y and the Nth row of the character.

As an example of how to use FNS the program below prints a character on the screen at 20,10 and then prints the value of the dot pattern that makes up each row of the character.

```
10 INPUT A$
20 MODE 4
30 PRINT TAB(20,10);A$
40 FOR N=0 TO 7
50 PRINT N,?FNS(20,10,N)
60 NEXT N
70 END
100 DEF FNS(X,Y,N)=HIMEM+(X+40*Y)*8+N
```

This program can also be used to discover how any character is made up – it was used to find out the values of the third row of blank, X and O, for example. In practice, the function FNS would typically be used in IF statements to decide what action a program should take according to what is stored at a particular location.

The character table and using the MOS to PEEK the screen

Although the BBC Micro doesn't use an external character

generator ROM, it still has to have a table of what dot patterns should be used to make each character somewhere in ROM. This character table can be found at the start of the MOS ROM, that is at address &C000. The dot pattern for each printable ASCII character is stored in this table as eight memory locations, each location corresponding to a row of dots. The first eight locations store the pattern for the ASCII blank, the next eight store the pattern for ! which is the next ASCII character and this sequence continues to the last printable ASCII character, ~. A short program to print the patterns stored in the character table is given below.

```
10  X=&C000
20  A=?X
30  PRINT ~X;TAB(15);FNB(A)
40  X=X+1
50  IF X=8*INT(X/8) THEN PRINT
60  GOTO 20

100 DEF FNB(X)
110 LOCAL I,A$
120 A$=""
130 FOR I=7 TO 0 STEP -1
140 A$=STR$(X-2*INT(X/2))+A$
150 X=INT(X/2)
160 NEXT I
170 =A$
```

The function FNB might be useful in other programs. It converts a number to a binary number and returns the result as a string. Whenever a character is to be printed on the screen the MOS looks up the dot pattern in the table and then stores it in the correct location in the screen memory. In two-colour modes this is straight-forward and only involves transferring the bit pattern as stored in the table. There is quite a lot more work to be done in four- and sixteen-colour modes. The bit pattern stored in the table has to be used to set groups of bits in as many as 32 memory locations to the current foreground colour. This is so complicated that it is better left to the MOS! However, knowledge of where the character table is located can be used to plot dots or print other letters in the correct pattern to form very large letter displays. Apart from this application the character table could be used in reverse to discover what character was displayed at any location on the screen. This would involve comparing each of the eight memory locations that make up the character on the screen with each block of eight locations of the character table that define a character until a match is found. This is a slow and fairly difficult procedure but fortunately the MOS contains a subroutine that will carry out the search for us.

The OSBYTE call (see Chapter Three) with A=&87 will return the ASCII code of the character currently under the text cursor. The following function FNASC(X,Y) will return the ASCII code at screen location X,Y and CHR$(FNASC(X,Y)) will supply the character itself:

```
100 DEF FNASC(X,Y)
110 LOCAL C
120 X%=X
130 Y%=Y
140 A%=135
150 C=USR(&FFF4)
160 C=C AND &FFFF
170 C=C DIV &100
180 =C
```

Finding the dot pattern corresponding to an ASCII code is fast because the table is organised so that the ASCII code leads straight to the correct pattern by a simple calculation. However, going back from the pattern to the ASCII code is slower because it involves finding a match for eight bytes somewhere in the table! Even so, the User Guide claims an average time of only 120 micro-seconds to find the character!

The 6845 video generator and the ULA video processor

Now that we have a fairly full picture of the way that information is stored in the video RAM it is time to reconsider the two major components of the video circuit – the 6845 video generator and the ULA video processor. If you recall the discussion in Chapter One, you will be aware that the 6845 is responsible for supplying the correct address of the memory location that contains the bit pattern of the row of dots that has to be displayed on the screen. For example, in mode 4 the first visible line of the TV frame is composed of the dot pattern in the first, eighth, sixteenth, etc. screen memory locations. In addition to generating these addresses it also produces the signals that provide the timing for the TV picture and a signal that is used to produce the cursor. The operation of the 6845 is controlled by the values stored in 18 internal registers. However, these internal registers cannot be accessed directly. Instead, the 6845 has a single *address register* and a single *data register*. To write a value to any of the internal registers you have to store the number of the register in the address register and then store the value in the data register. To read a value from any register, the same procedure is followed except of course that the data register is read. In the BBC Micro, the 6845's address register is at &FE00 and its data register is at &FE01. The MOS provides a way of storing information in the 6845's internal register using the statement VDU 23,0,R,X,0,0,0,0,0,0 where R is the register number and X is the value to be stored in it. To read the value stored in a register there is no choice but to use ?&FE00=reg and ?&FE01=value. You could use the 18 registers to change the mode of operation of the 6845 to produce different screen formats but because the BASIC and MOS expect to work with the particular formats corresponding to modes 0 to 7 there are lots of problems unless you intend to handle every screen function yourself. A table of 6845 registers with brief comments is given below just to give you some idea of the sort of things that can be changed. If you are really interested in using the 6845 in 'odd' ways then my advice is to get hold of a full data sheet.

Table 4.1   6845 registers

Register	Comments
R0	The total time taken for each horizontal scan line i.e. the horizontal sync frequency.
R1	The number of characters on a line.
R2	Position of horizontal sync pulse.
R3	Width of horizontal sync pulse.
R4	Vertical sync frequency.
R5	Vertical sync frequency.
R6	Number of character lines displayed.
R7	Vertical sync position.
R8	Interlace mode.
R9	No. of vertical dots per character.
R10	Cursor start line.
R11	Cursor stop line.
R12	(LSB) used with register 13 to specify the memory location corresponding to the first character location.
R13	(MSB) see R12.
R14	With R15 holds the address of the cursor.
R15	See R14.
R16	Light pen register.
R17	Light pen register.

The few registers that are useful to the user are made available via the MOS. For example, R14 and R15 are used by the OSBYTE call with A=86 to read the current cursor position. The cursor control registers 10 and 11 are used by VDU 23,1,0;0;0;0 which turns the cursor off and VDU 23,1,1;0;0;0;0 which restores it.

The 6845 is responsible for providing the address of the memory locations in the correct order but it is the ULA video processor that is responsible for taking the contents of the memory and converting them to dots of the correct colour. As always, it is easier to consider the two-colour case of mode 4 first. At each access a memory location provides eight bits but the TV display requires these eight bits one at a time in the correct order as the scan builds up a line across the screen. The ULA takes the eight bits from memory and feeds them out one after the other. In other words, it serialises the bits. If this was all the ULA did the BBC Micro's graphics facility would be severely limited. The video output of the video processor consists of the three signals R (Red), G (Green) and B (Blue). The colour displayed on the screen depends on which of the outputs are 'on'. For example, R on and G on produces a yellow output. All three being on produces white. You should be able to see that by taking all combinations of G and B you can produce eight different colours.

Table 4.2 Three-bit colour codes
(N.B. 1 = on).

CODE	BGR	Colour
0	000	Black
1	001	Red
2	010	Green
3	011	Yellow
4	100	Blue
5	101	Magenta
6	110	Cyan
7	111	White

Now consider the problem of determining the colour of a dot displayed on the screen. In a two-colour mode each bit coming out of the serialiser could be used to select one of the eight possible colours. The only sensible way to do this is to have an extra small memory, called the *palette*, that is used to store a code for the colour to be produced when the bit is a one and another code for when the bit is a zero. The easiest code to use is a three-bit representation of which of RGB are on and which are off, as shown in Table 4.2.

Suppose, for example, that the palette has just two memory locations whose addresses are zero and one and that the code 011 is stored in zero and 101 is stored in one. Then if the output of the serialiser is fed to the palette as an address, a zero bit will produce a colour code of 011 and a one bit will produce 101. In other words, a yellow background with magenta dots will be displayed. By changing the colour codes stored in the palette any two of the eight colours can be used in a two-colour mode.

This idea extends quite easily to the four- and sixteen-colour modes. In the four-colour case we need a palette memory with four locations addressed as 00, 01, 10 and 11, each location again being capable of storing three bits of information. Now each dot on the screen is determined by two bits and this is reflected in the workings of the serialiser. Instead of changing each byte into a single stream of bits it changes each byte into two streams of bits. This is done in such a way that at any moment the two bits coming out of the serialiser are the correct two bits to determine the colour of a single dot. These two bits are used to address the palette and hence are converted into the colour codes. Obviously the four colours that appear on the screen can be selected from any of the eight available colours.

The sixteen-colour mode works in exactly the same way, the only problem being that there are only eight colours! The solution is that the extra eight colours are not really colours at all. They are just combinations of the original eight colours flashing. The palette can in fact store four bits not just the three RGB bits. The fourth bit is a *flash bit* in the sense that if it is 1 then the colour displayed on the screen alternates between its code value as stored in the palette and colour corresponding to its code value with all bits inverted. For example, if the palette held 1101, the flash bit would be set and the colour displayed would alternate between 101, magenta, and 010, green. In a sixteen-colour mode the serialiser feeds four streams of bits to be used as an address to a palette with sixteen memory locations.

After all this description it is worth summarising the details of the palette and the serialiser. The palette is a small area of memory within the video processor. Each location within the palette can store four bits which correspond to flash, B, G and R and whose state determines which of the sixteen colours is produced on the screen. The serialiser changes each byte retrieved from the video memory into either one, two or four streams of bits depending on whether the mode is a two-, four- or sixteen-colour mode. The bits forming these streams are used to address the palette RAM and so the colour codes stored in the video RAM are converted to actual colours. The relationship between the serialiser and the palette is shown in Figure 4.8.

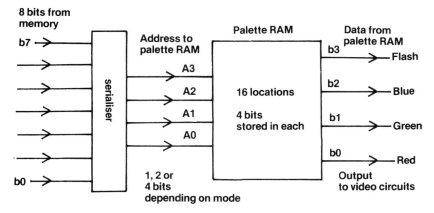

Fig. 4.8. The serialiser and palette RAM.

This changing of the colour codes stored in the video RAM to the actual colour codes produced by the palette is represented in the BBC Micro's software by the idea of *logical* and *actual* colour. Within each mode the same logical colour codes are always used. In a two-colour mode these are 0 and 1, in a four-colour mode they are 0,1,2,3 and in a sixteen-colour mode they are 0 to 15. In each case these codes are simply the result of the number of bits used to control the colour of a dot in each mode; at this stage they have nothing to do with colour. They are associated with actual colours by the contents of the palette RAM. For example, if in a four-colour mode the third location of the palette RAM contained 0110, then the logical code 3 (11 in binary) would produce a cyan dot. The contents of the palette RAM can be changed by the VDU 19 command. The form of this command is:

VDU 19,logical colour,actual colour,0,0,0

which causes 'logical colour' to produce 'actual colour' on the screen. Another way of looking at this command is that it stores the code for the actual colour in the location in the palette RAM with the address given by the code for the logical colour. For example, VDU 19,1,2,0,0,0 sets logical colour 1 to actual colour 2, i.e. green, or it stores the code 0010 in the palette RAM location 01 depending on how you look at it!

To read the current contents of the palette RAM you can use an OSWORD call with A=&0B. This is described on page 462 of the User Guide and needs no further comment.

Hardware scrolling

There is one feature of the BBC Micro that is very surprising and can make use of the screen address map very difficult. When you carry out a MODE command the screen address map is set up as we have discussed and remains unaltered during the running of a program unless that program prints something that causes the screen to scroll. The action of scrolling is such a common sight on VDUs and computers that it is rare to give it a second thought. However, if you try to write a program from first principles that will scroll an entire screen you will realise what a time-consuming manoeuvre it is. Each text line of the screen must be moved up by one line. The bottom line is cleared and the top line is lost. In the BBC Micro's case, this screen shift for mode 4, if done by software, would need 10K bytes of storage to be rearranged. This would be slow, to say the least. To overcome this speed problem, scrolling is carried out by hardware which, in effect, alters the screen memory map so that the memory locations correspond to screen positions one higher. The memory corresponding to the old top line is cleared and is made to correspond to the new bottom line. In other words, following a single scroll, POKEing data into memory that was the top line produces output on the bottom line. Of course this *re-mapping* of the screen makes a non-sense of the screen mapping functions given earlier! The solution is simple – either avoid scrolling the screen following a MODE command or adjust the functions to take account of any scrolling.

To take account of scrolling it is necessary to keep a count of the number of times the screen has scrolled since the last MODE command. If the scroll count is kept in SC then the following version of FNS will work (for mode 4):

```
100 DEF FNS(X,Y,N)
110 YT=Y+SC
120 YT=YT-INT(ABS(YT)/32)*32
130 =HIMEM+(X+Y*40)*8+N
```

Notice that YT and SC are global variables and are accessible to the main program. Luckily, it is not often that the need to scroll the screen occurs in the same situation as the need to use POKE or PEEK graphics.

The way that the scrolling hardware works is quite simple. The 6845 video generator chip contains two registers, R12 and R13, which hold the address (divided by 8) of the start of the video RAM. These registers are set to the normal start of the screen following a MODE statement. However, when a scroll occurs the starting address held in the registers is increased so as to point to the start of the second line of the screen. This now becomes the new top line and every other line is moved up one. But what about the bottom line? It is now below the start of the area of memory that is displayed and so will not appear on the screen? The BBC Micro has some special electronics to overcome this problem. No matter where it starts from, the video generator always tries to display the same amount of RAM. As the highest video RAM address is always the same in any mode (&7FFF in a 32K machine and &3FFF in a 16K machine) an address produced by the video generator above the top of the video RAM area can easily be detected. When the screen display is in its initial state the video generator addresses memory from the start of the video RAM right up to the top. However, following even a single scroll, it will overshoot the top of the video RAM by exactly the amount that it has moved up. This is detected by the BBC Micro and a number is added to any such address to bring it back to the start of the video RAM. In other words, the address is made to *wrap round* the video RAM. This means that the previous top line isn't lost; it is now displayed (after being cleared) as the new bottom line. The number to be added to such out-of-range addresses is different for each mode and is set by the state of the two lines C1 and C2 from VIA–A (see Chapter One).

The consequences of this hardware scrolling method are that you can set the starting point of the screen display lower by changing the values stored in R12 and R13 without any trouble but trying to increase it causes the screen to scroll. Only in this case the scroll is really a *screen* roll because the lines that appear at the bottom are not cleared first! By changing the contents of R12 and R13 by less than a whole line you can implement horizontal screen rolls. Try experimenting with the following program:

```
10 MODE 4
20 CLS
30 PRINT TAB(15,10);"HI THERE"
40 S%=HIMEM/8
50 VDU 23,0,13,I%+S% AND &00FF,0,0,0,0,0,0
60 I%=I%+1
70 IF I%>39 THEN I%=0
80 FOR J%=1 TO 1000:NEXT J%
90 GOTO 50
```

There is an easy way of disabling hardware scrolling and that is to define a text window using VDU 28. If a text window is defined then it is possible that not *all* of the screen will have to be scrolled. Because of this the hardware cannot be used and each line must be moved up by a software transfer. If you try this you will realise how valuable hardware scrolling is in speeding things up!

Mode 7 teletext graphics

A Mode 7 display works in a completely different way from any of the other modes. Instead of storing the bit pattern corresponding to the shape of each character to be displayed, only the ASCII code is stored. The actual bit pattern for each character is stored in an extra ROM in the video circuitry. You should recognise this as the 'classical' video circuit described at the beginning of this chapter. The only difference is that the ROM, an SAA 5050 teletext generator, produces three output signals R (Red), G (Green) and B (Blue) for an eight-colour display (with certain limitations). The advantage of using this classical arrangement is that it provides a 40 character by 25 line display using only 1K of RAM. Even though only 1K of RAM is used, mode 7 provides a full upper and lower case character set and a low resolution (80 by 75) in colour! However, even though mode 7 can solve many graphics problems in less space than the other modes, it isn't used as often as it could be. The main reason for this is that the colour control in mode 7 is by the use of control codes and the graphics take the form of *block graphics characters*. These are both more difficult and more restrictive than the methods used in the other modes. However, with a little understanding and practice mode 7 can be used to produce very good effects. To see the sort of results that can be achieved just look at any of the broadcast teletext pages.

As already mentioned, only the ASCII codes of the characters on the screen are stored in RAM in mode 7. This means that changing the contents of a single memory location will change the dot pattern for an entire character location. The memory map in mode 7 is:

```
memory location = HIMEM+X+Y*40
```

which is the address of the memory location corresponding to the character at X,Y. To see this in action try the following:

```
10 FOR X=0 TO 39
20 FOR Y=0 TO 24
30 ?FNS(X,Y)=ASC("A")
40 NEXT Y
50 NEXT X
60 STOP
70 DEF FNS(X,Y)=HIMEM+X+40*Y
```

Notice the use of the ASC function to store the ASCII code for the letter A in the memory location. You can use the FNS function to examine and change screen locations in mode 7 but OSBYTE call with A=&87 (see earlier) is likely to be just as fast in this case.

The colour of teletext graphics is set by the use of control codes rather than COLOUR or GCOL statements. These codes are easy to use in that they set the colour of all the teletext characters that follow until another code or a new line removes their effect. However, there is one problem in that they are not invisible on the screen. Every control code shows on the screen as a blank character the same colour as the current background. This makes changing colours in mid-line impossible without leaving a space between the two coloured zones the same colour as the current background. In other words, two areas of different foreground colours cannot meet on a line. There is, however, nothing stopping two lines of different foreground colours 'touching'. Even with this restriction it is still possible to draw very good teletext pictures. As mentioned earlier, the best way to discover more is to study the transmitted teletext pictures on the BBC (television!).

Conclusion

This chapter has tried to explore some of the hardware and software aspects of the BBC Micro's graphics capabilities. It has, however, barely scratched the surface of this vast topic. In particular, no mention has been made of the standard BASIC and MOS commands, such as PLOT and VDU. These are well described in the User Guide, although, of course, there is a lot to be learned through experimentation and general experience. The practical value of the information presented in this chapter about graphics memory maps for the different modes will be considered in Chapter Eight where we consider the problem of writing a screen dump program.

Chapter Five
The Sound Generator

One of the attractions of the BBC Micro as a machine to have fun with is the presence of a sound generator chip with one noise channel and three tone channels. Just this hardware alone would lead you to expect to be able to produce three note chords and a range of simple sound effects. However, the software that is built into the MOS and the BASIC to handle it makes it a lot more powerful than the hardware specification might lead you to believe. By the clever use of interrupts and a system of queues the BBC Micro can make sounds and move things around the screen, etc. at the same time! In addition, the ENVELOPE command gives the BASIC programmer an amazingly high degree of control over the nature of the sound produced. Once again, the combination of good hardware enhanced by well thought out software makes the BBC Micro remarkable!

In this chapter we will take a closer look at the sound generator and the sound generating software inside the BBC Micro. Some of the discussion will be about the sound generator hardware itself and this will be of particular interest to the assembly language programmer. However, the first part of the chapter deals with the software – the SOUND and ENVELOPE commands – how they work and what they can be used for.

An overview

Before becoming too deeply involved in the details of using the sound generator it is worth taking an overview of the facilities it provides. There are three tone generators that can be used to produce either single notes or up to three-note chords. There is, in addition, a single noise channel that can produce eight different effects. This fairly simple hardware is controlled using two extensions to BASIC – SOUND and ENVELOPE. The SOUND command is the only one of the pair that actually causes anything to come out of the tiny speaker just above the keyboard. Among other things, it controls the pitch, amplitude and duration of the notes produced. The ENVELOPE command is used to change the characteristics of the notes produced by the SOUND command. Used without the ENVELOPE command, SOUND produces a more or less pure tone with a given frequency, which is fine for most applications, e.g. beeps during games or playing simple tunes. However, if you want to try to produce more complicated sounds then you have to use the ENVELOPE command to alter the basic sound produced. There are two general reasons for wanting to produce more complex noises – either you are interested in music and making your BBC Micro sound like a piano, a flute, an organ, a guitar ... or you want to make especially convincing sound effects such as a police siren, a gun shot, etc.

The study of the BBC Micro's sound capabilities, therefore, falls into these two categories – music and sound effects.

There are three levels of difficulty involved in making music with the BBC Micro:

1. Playing simple tunes.
2. Playing music with three-part harmony.
3. *Synthesising* the sound of other instruments.

The first two involve the use of only the SOUND command but the last one also needs a mastery of the ENVELOPE command. To get very far with any of the three you also need a reasonable understanding of music but if you feel a little unsure about this then programming sound is a very enjoyable way to learn.

The subject of sound effects is much more limited because all that we are trying to do is to compile a catalogue of 'recipes' to make a few standard noises. However, there are two ways of approaching sound effects. You can either use the SOUND command to control the noise channel or you can use the ENVELOPE command to define basic sounds. With the latter you can produce quite remarkable effects but there's still a great deal of scope for producing a wide variety of noises using the SOUND command, and it can fill the requirements of most games playing applications alone.

The SOUND command

The SOUND command has the general form

SOUND C,A,P,D

where C controls which channel – 0 (the noise channel), 1, 2 or 3 – produces the sound; A controls the volume and ranges from 0 (silence) to −15 (loudest); P controls the pitch of the note and ranges from 0 (lowest pitch) to 255 (highest); and D controls the duration of the note and ranges from 1 to 255 in twentieths of a second. (However, it is worth noticing that if D is set to −1 then the note produced will continue to sound until you take steps to stop it!) There are various extra meanings associated with the parameters C and A. Positive values of A in the range 1 to 4 cause the pitch and volume of the note to be controlled by the parameters of an ENVELOPE command. The channel parameter C is in fact quite complicated and is best thought of as a four-digit hexadecimal number

&HSFN

where each of the letters stands for a digit that controls a different aspect of sound production. What exactly each of them does is better left until later except to say that N is the channel number as described earlier.

Programming tunes is simply a matter of converting notes into numbers. This is easy once you know that middle C corresponds to a value of 53 and going up or down by a whole tone corresponds to adding or subtracting 8. The only thing that you have to be careful to remember is that there isn't always a whole tone between two notes. For example, between the notes of C and D there is a whole tone but between E and F there is only a semi-tone. The pattern of tones and semi-tones from C to C an octave above is

$$C-D-E-F-G-A-B-C$$
$$T\quad T\quad S\quad T\quad T\quad T\quad S$$

which is easy to remember because it's the same as the pattern of white and black notes on the piano. Obviously, sharps and flats can be produced by adding or subtracting 4. So you can produce the full chromatic scale by

```
10 FOR P=53 TO 97 STEP 4
20 SOUND 1,-15,P,10
30 NEXT P
```

This short program can also be used to demonstrate a unique feature of the BBC Micro. If you add line 15:

```
15 PRINT P
```

you will discover that the numbers are printed on the screen and even though the program finishes, the sound keeps on coming. The reason for this remarkable behaviour is that the BBC Micro maintains a queue of sounds that are produced one after the other as soon as the current sound is completed. The sound queue is processed independently of any BASIC program that is running and each SOUND statement simply adds a note to the end of the queue. This means that a BASIC program isn't held up for the duration of each note. The only time that this fails is when the queue becomes full and a SOUND statement tries to add another note to it. The result is that the program then has to wait until the end of the currently sounding note when the queue is reduced by one and the SOUND statement can add its note. There is a separate queue for each channel and each can hold up to four notes.

Programming tunes

To make a tune recognisable, not only must it have each note at the right pitch, each note must also last for the correct time. The normal system of musical notation is based on repeatedly dividing a time interval by two to obtain shorter notes so it is a good idea to include a variable in all music programs that sets the length of the fundamental unit of time. As an example of programming a simple tune consider the first few notes of *Hearts of Oak* (see Figure 5.1). Translating each note to its pitch and duration value for the SOUND statement gives the two rows of numbers under the music in Figure 5.1. The best way to convert these numbers to sound is to use a DATA statement thus:

```
 5 C=5
10 DATA 69,1,89,1,89,.75,89,.25,89,1,105,.75,
   97,.25,89,1,85,.75,77,.25,69,.75,99,99
20 READ P,D
30 IF P=99 THEN STOP
40 SOUND 1,-15,P,D*C
50 SOUND 1,1,P,2
60 GOTO 20
```

Line 50 has the effect of leaving short silences between each of the notes. Without this line all the notes run together. Try deleting it and re-running the program to appreciate the effect – it is one that you'd want to use to 'slur' notes. You can program any tunes that you have music for in the same way.

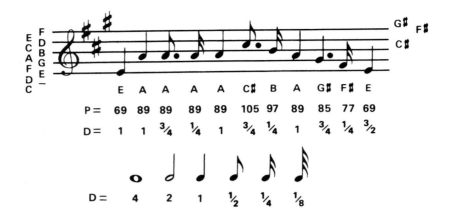

A ● FOLLOWING A NOTE INCREASES D BY 50%

Fig. 5.1. The first few notes of *Hearts of Oak* and their digital values for the SOUND command. (Reprinted by permission of *Computing Today*.)

Three note chords

Most home computers with a sound generator could manage the simple tune given in the last section. What is special about the BBC Micro is that it is possible to generate three notes at the same time. To see how this sounds, try the following:

```
10 DIM N(13)
20 DATA 53,61,69,73,81,89,99,101,109,117,
        121,129,137
30 FOR I=1 TO 13
40 READ N(I)
50 NEXT I
60 A$=INKEY$(0)
70 IF A$="" THEN GOTO 60
80 A=VAL(A$)
90 SOUND 1,-15,N(A),20
100 SOUND 2,-15,N(A+2),20
110 SOUND 3,-15,N(A+4),20
120 GOTO 60
```

If you RUN this program, by pressing each of the keys 1 to 8 you will be able to hear the eight chords produced by adding a third and a fifth to each of the notes of the scale of C. (A third is a musical interval corresponding to playing a note two notes higher up the scale and a fifth corresponds to playing a note four notes higher up.) This is the simplest kind of chord, called a *triad*, and is very pleasing to the ear. Typing in almost any combination of the number keys 1 to 9 will produce something tuneful and it is easy to sit at your BBC Micro and produce music. For example, if you want to hear a snatch of tune that is almost recognisable try typing in the following sequence.

5 5 6 6 4 5 7 7 8 7 6 5

No prizes for guessing this one! The array N is used to hold the pitch values for the notes of the scale of C and enough notes higher up to form the triad on B. You can write a program to play a piece of music with up to three-note chords using the same method as given for the single melody in the last section.

There is one thing wrong with the previous program and that is that each note of the chord starts at a slightly different time. In other words, each of the SOUND commands starts off its note in the chord as soon as it is reached. As they are executed one after another, the note on channel 1 starts a little before that on channel 2, which starts a little before that on channel 3. The solution to this problem would be to tell the sound generator to wait for two other notes after the one initiated by line 90 before making any noise at all. This is the purpose of the S part of the channel parameter introduced in the section about the form of the SOUND command. If you use a non-zero value for S, the sound generator will wait for other notes before it starts playing. The number of notes that it waits for is given by the value of S and the SOUND commands that produce them must also use the same value of S. For example, in the case of the triads played by the previous program the SOUND commands would be replaced by

```
 90 SOUND &0201,-15,N(A),20
100 SOUND &0202,-15,N(A),20
110 SOUND &0203,-15,N(A+4),20
```

The first SOUND command has a value of S equal to 2 so the sound generator waits for two more SOUND commands with S set to 2 before producing a chord made up of all three notes.

The other parts of the channel parameter are also concerned with the timing of notes. The H part of the parameter can either be a 0 or a 1. If it is a 1, it adds a dummy note to the sound queue that allows any previous notes to continue without being cut short by another note. This really only makes any sense when used with the ENVELOPE command. The F part can be either 0 or 1 and if it is 1 it causes any notes stored in the channel's queue to be removed or 'flushed' and the note specified by the current SOUND command to be produced immediately. This is useful for cutting short sound effects and starting new ones, sychronised with external effects. For example, in a graphics game you might want to stop the noise of a fire gun and replace it by an explosion.

Simple sound effects

The only sound channel that we haven't discussed as yet is the noise channel – Channel 0. The noise produced by this channel depends on the value of the pitch parameter P in the SOUND command:

Value of P	*Noise*
0	High frequency periodic.
1	Medium frequency periodic.
2	Low frequency periodic.
3	Periodic of a frequency set by channel 1.
4	High frequency 'white' noise.
5	Medium frequency 'white' noise.
6	Low frequency 'white' noise.
7	Noise of frequency set by channel 1.

The first three noises (P=0 to 2) are rasping noises that come in very handy for 'losing' noises in games! Values of P between 4 and 6 produce hissing noises of various frequencies. White noise is a special sort of hissing noise that is made up by mixing a note of every pitch in much the same way that white light is made up by mixing light of every colour.

There isn't very much that you can do to change the nature of the sounds produced when P has a value of 0,1,2,4,5 or 6 apart from altering the volume and duration. However, by changing only these two parameters and combining noises you can still produce a useful range of effects. For example, if you make any noise very short it begins to sound *percussive* (like something being hit) and if you combine a very short burst of white noise with a very short high pitched tone you produce a noise like a metallic click. Try:

```
10 SOUND 0,-15,4,1:SOUND 1,-15,200,1
```

Similarly, mixing two noise-like sounds produces new effects. So, for example:

```
10 SOUND 0,-15,4,1:SOUND 0,-15,3,1
20 GOTO 10
```

produces a sound like a machine gun. Notice that as this example uses the same channel twice, the two sounds follow each other to give a rhythmical pulsing sound. Using this idea with two different pitches of 'white' noise produces a sound very like a helicopter:

```
10 SOUND 0,-15,4,2
20 SOUND 0,-15,5,1
30 GOTO 10
```

Notice that one of the sounds has to be twice as long to give the pulsating beat of a helicopter's rotor blades. You can go on experimenting like this indefinitely! The range of sounds that can be produced using channel 0 alone is so great that discovering new sounds is easy. Putting a name to them is quite a different problem!

The pitch values 3 and 7 are special because they produce noises on channel 0 that are controlled by the pitch on channel 1. This opens the door to sound effects that involve noises that change in pitch. For example.

```
10 SOUND 0,-15,7,55
20 FOR I=200 TO 255
30 SOUND 1,0,I,1
40 NEXT I
```

produces a noise like a space ship taking off. The pitch of the noise on channel 0 started by line 10 is continuously changed by line 30. Notice that using a volume of 0 means that the notes produced by line 30 are silent! Finally, try:

```
10 SOUND 0,-15,7,55
20 SOUND 1,0,200,1
30 SOUND 1,0,255,1
40 GOTO 20
```

which produces a sound like a car engine being started (or rather failing to start!)

The ENVELOPE command

The ENVELOPE command is a very sophisticated way of controlling the output of the sound generator. Without it there would be no way of producing really complicated sounds without resorting to assembly language. Part of the trouble with understanding the way an ENVELOPE command produces a sound is that it is always used in conjunction with a SOUND command and it is these two commands together that determine the actual sound produced.

The ENVELOPE command is fairly difficult to use because it has so many different parameters and because it is difficult to see how these parameters are used to produce any desired sound. The User Guide goes into some detail about what each of the parameters actually does but it is still worth pointing out the general principle behind the operation of the ENVELOPE command.

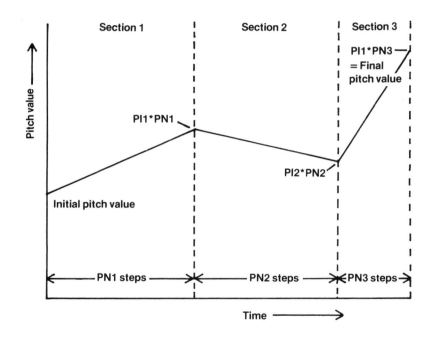

Fig. 5.2. Pitch graph.

Using the notation defined on page 245 of the User Guide, the format of an ENVELOPE command is:

ENVELOPE N,T,PI1,PI2,PI3,PN1,PN2,PN3,
                AA,AD,AS,AR,ALA,ALD

Broadly speaking, there are two types of parameter in an ENVELOPE command – pitch parameters and amplitude parameters. The pitch parameters control the variation in pitch (if any) that occur and the amplitude parameters control any variation in volume that occurs. You can think of these two sets of parameters as defining two graphs – a graph of pitch with time and a graph of amplitude with time. The way that the pitch parameters determine the pitch graph can be seen in Figure 5.2. The three parts of the pitch graph are each controlled by two parameters. PN1 to PN3 set the number of steps in each section and PI1 to PI3 set the change in the pitch value for each step in each of the sections. There are two pieces of information missing from this graph. We also need to know how long each step lasts for and the starting pitch value. The first requirement is met by the parameter T, which specifies the duration of each step in hundredths of a second. The initial pitch value is set by the pitch value in the SOUND command that refers to the envelope. It is possible that the total time specified for the pitch graph, i.e. (PN1+PN2+PN3)×step duration, is shorter than the time that the note sounds for. In this case one of two things can happen. If bit 7 of the T parameter is a one, then the pitch value remains at the final value specified by the graph for the rest of the sound. However, if bit 7 of T is zero then the pitch value returns to the initial value and the whole pitch graph is used repeatedly until the sound ends. Thus the parameter T conveys two pieces of information, the duration of a step and whether the pitch graph should 'auto repeat'.

The way that the amplitude parameters specify the amplitude graph can be seen in Figure 5.3. The amplitude graph is a little more difficult to follow than the pitch graph because the time that each section lasts isn't explicitly stated. The attack section comes to an end when the amplitude reaches the specified attack level, ALA. During this period the amplitude, which always starts at zero unless continuing a previous note, increases or decreases by an amount given in AA at each step. The attack section is followed by the decay section. During this period the amplitude increases or decreases by an amount specified by AS at each step until it reaches the final decay level specified in ALD. Notice that the times of the attack and decay sections are not specified directly. Instead, each section lasts until the amplitude reaches the specified final value. However, it is easy to work out how long each lasts:

$$\text{Attack period} = \frac{\text{ALA}}{\text{AA}} \times \text{step duration}$$

$$\text{Decay period} = \frac{\text{ALD}}{\text{AD}} \times \text{step duration}$$

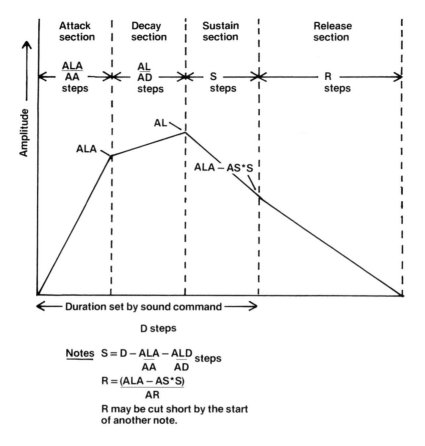

Fig. 5.3. Amplitude graph.

The time that the third section – the sustain section – lasts isn't set by the ENVELOPE command. The overall time that the note lasts is set by the duration specified in the SOUND command that makes use of the envelope. The sustain section lasts for however much time the note has left to sound after the attack and decay sections. During this period the amplitude decreases by an amount specified in AS at each step. The final section of the graph – the release section – is the strangest of all in that it happens after the 'official' end of the note as set by the duration in the SOUND command. If the note isn't followed immediately by another then the amplitude continues to fall by an amount specified in AR at each step. The note finally terminates because the amplitude reaches zero or because another note starts.

Experimenting with ENVELOPE

The above description of how the ENVELOPE command works is
all very well but how do you specify the values of the parameters to
produce a sound of your choice? There is no easy answer to this
question. Sounds have to be constructed by trial and error. To aid in
this process the following program allows the parameters of an
ENVELOPE command to be changed one at a time and the result
heard.

```
 10 MODE 4
 20 PROCINIT
 30 PROCPRINT
 40 PROCCHANGE
 50 GOTO 40
 60 STOP

 70 DEF PROCPRINT
 80 CLS
 90 @%=&00020205:PRINT TAB(10);
    "(T) Time unit=";T/100;" s"
100 PRINT:PRINT TAB(10);"Frequency Section"
110 PRINT:@%=10
120 PRINT "(P1) Repeat =";R$
130 PRINT "(P2) Change in pitch section 1
    =";PI1
140 PRINT "(P3) Number of steps in section 1
    =";PN1
150 PRINT "(P4) Change in pitch section 2
    =";PI2
160 PRINT "(P5) Number of steps in section 2
    =";PN2
170 PRINT "(P6) Change in pitch section 3
    =";PI3
180 PRINT "(P7) Number of steps in section 3
    =";PN3
190 PRINT "(P8) Initial Pitch= ";P
200 PRINT
210 PRINT TAB(10);"Amplitude Section"
220 PRINT
230 PRINT "(A1) Attack rate of change =";AA;
    "per step"
240 PRINT "(A2) Attack target level   =";ALA
250 PRINT "(A3) Decay rate of change  =";AD;
    "per step"
260 PRINT "(A4) Decay target level    =";ALD
270 PRINT "(A5) Sustain rate of change=";AS;
    "per step"
280 PRINT "(A6) Release rate of change=";AR
290 PRINT
```

```
300 PRINT "(D) Total Duration =";D/20;
    "s (=";D/20/T*100;" steps)"
310 PRINT TAB(5,28);"Press S to hear sound"
320 ENDPROC

330 DEF PROCINIT
340 T=1
350 R$="OFF":R=1
360 PI1=0
370 PI2=0
380 PI3=0
390 PN1=0
400 PN2=0
410 PN3=0
420 P=128
430 AA=10
440 AD=-10
450 AS=-20
460 AR=-10
470 ALA=100
480 ALD=10
490 D=5
500 ENDPROC

510 DEF PROCSOUND
520 ENVELOPE 1,T+128*R,PI1,PI2,PI3,PN1,PN2,
    PN3,AA,AD,AS,AR,ALA,ALD
530 SOUND 1,1,P,D
540 ENDPROC

550 DEF PROCCHANGE
560 A$=INKEY$(0)
570 IF A$="" THEN GOTO 560
580 IF A$="S" THEN PROCSOUND:GOTO 560
590 IF A$="T" THEN PRINT TAB(2,30);
    "Time unit (in secs)= ";:INPUT T:T=T*100
600 IF A$="D" THEN PRINT TAB(2,30);
    "Total Duration (in secs)= ";:INPUT D:D=D*20
610 IF A$="P" THEN PROCPITCH:GOTO 560
620 IF A$="A" THEN PROCAMP:GOTO 560
630 PROCPRINT
640 GOTO 560

650 DEF PROCPITCH
660 A$=INKEY$(0)
670 IF A$<"0" OR A$>"9" THEN GOTO 660
680 A=EVAL(A$)
690 IF A=1 THEN GOTO 790
700 PRINT TAB(2,30);"Pitch parameter ";A;
    " = ";:INPUT P
710 IF A=2 THEN PI1=PP
720 IF A=3 THEN PN1=PP
730 IF A=4 THEN PI2=PP
```

```
740 IF A=5 THEN PN2=PP
750 IF A=6 THEN PI3=PP
760 IF A=7 THEN PN3=PP
770 IF A=8 THEN P=PP
780 GOTO 810
790 PRINT TAB(2,30);"Repeat ON or OFF";
    :INPUT R$
800 IF R$="ON" THEN R=0 ELSE R=1
810 PROCPRINT
820 ENDPROC

830 DEF PROCAMP
840 A$=INKEY$(0)
850 IF A$<"0" OR A$>"9" THEN GOTO 840
860 A=EVAL(A$)
870 PRINT TAB(2,30);"Amplitude parameter ";A;
    " = ";:INPUT PP
880 IF A=1 THEN AA=PP
890 IF A=2 THEN ALA=PP
900 IF A=3 THEN AD=PP
910 IF A=4 THEN ALD=PP
920 IF A=5 THEN AS=PP
930 IF A=6 THEN AR=PP
940 PROCPRINT
950 ENDPROC
```

The procedure PROCINIT sets initial values to all the
ENVELOPE and SOUND parameters. PROCPRINT prints a list
of all the parameters, their meaning and their current value.
PROCCHANGE can be used to change the value of any of the
parameters by typing the parameter's code (written in brackets on
the left by PROCPRINT). To hear the sound, simply press S. Using
this program you can construct and adjust sound effects very easily.
Once you have the sound that you want, write down the final values
for all the parameters and use them in ENVELOPE and SOUND
commands in your own programs.

The sound generator hardware

The sound generator chip used in the BBC Micro is a SN 76489 bus-
controlled sound generator. This chip was designed to be used
directly with microprocessors. However, if you recall the discussion
in Chapter One of the way that VIA-A is used as a slow data bus to
various peripherals including the sound generator chip you will
realise that it is not interfaced directly to the 6502's data or address
bus. The SN 76489 has eight data inputs, two control inputs and one
control output. The eight data lines are directly connected to the A

side of VIA-A. Only one of the control lines is actually used and this is the WE (write enable) line. This is connected to output 0 of the 74LS259 addressable latch. The WE line must be *low* (i.e. logic zero) before any data is transferred to the sound generator. Thus the sequence to write a single byte of information to the chip is:

1. Set the A side of VIA-A to outputs and store the data in the data register.
2. Set the WE line to logic zero. As WE is connected to output zero of the addressable latch this is achieved by setting bits 0 to 3 of the B side of VIA-A to zero, taking care not to alter the state of any of the other bits in the B side data register.
3. After 32 clock pulses the data will have been read in to the chip and the WE line must be returned to one. This is done by setting bit 4 of the B side of VIA-A to one. After this, the sound generator chip is ready for the next byte.

This procedure may seem complicated but it is very easy to write a BASIC procedure to transfer bytes to the sound generator:

```
1000 DEF PROCSOUND(BYTE%)
1010 LOCAL VIA%,TEMP%
1020 VIA%=&FE40
1030 VIA%?&3=&FF
1040 VIA%?&F=BYTE%
1050 TEMP%=?VIA%
1060 ?VIA%=(TEMP% AND &F0)
1090 ?VIA%=(TEMP% AND &F8)
1100 ?VIA%=TEMP%
1110 ENDPROC
```

Line 1020 sets VIA% to the address of VIA-A. Line 1030 sets VIA-A's A side to outputs (see Chapter Six for more explanation of the VIA's control registers). Line 1040 stores the data in the data register and lines 1060 and 1090 change the WE line to zero and then back to one. Notice the use of line 1050 and the variable TEMP% to avoid altering the state of any other of the outputs. The only part of the procedure that is left to chance is the time between setting the WE line to zero and then back again to one. As BASIC is slow compared to the 4 MHz clock rate fed to the sound generator chip it is safe to assume that at least 32 clock pulses occur between line 1060 and 1090. If you convert this procedure into an assembly language routine then it would be necessary to add a pause while the 32 clock pulses happened.

The only extra information necessary to control the sound

generator is the format of the data bytes. This is easier to understand after looking a little more at how the sound generator chip works.

Each of the tone generators takes the form of a 10-bit counter connected to a four-stage attenuator. The output of each attenuator is summed together to produce the audio signal (see Figure 5.4). The

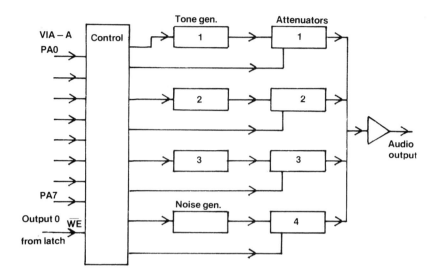

Fig. 5.4. Block diagram of SN76489AN sound generator.

counter is decremented once every 16 clock pulses and whenever it reaches zero its output to the attenuator changes state, i.e. if it was a high it will go low and vice versa. To set the frequency of the output signal the counter can be loaded with a 10-bit binary number which is reloaded automatically each time the counter reaches zero. Thus, the frequency of the square wave that is fed to the attenuator is given by:

$$f = \frac{N}{32n}$$

where N is the input clock frequency in Hz and n is the 10-bit binary number. (On the BBC Micro, N=4 MHz.) Each stage of the four-stage attenuator can be switched on and off individually. The stages give 2dB, 4dB, 8dB and 16dB attenuation and selecting all four stages turns the output of the tone generator off. Obviously, specifying the attenuation requires four bits, one for each stage. The noise generator is also connected to the audio output via a four-stage attenuator. The noise generator itself takes the form of a shift register with a feedback loop that can either be configured to produce a roughly periodic signal or a sequence of pseudo-random bits. The pseudo-random sequence when fed into the audio signal is a good approximation to *white noise* – a sound that should contain all frequencies at the same time! In addition the rate at which the shift register is clocked can be set to one of three preset frequencies or the output of tone generator three can be used.

The sound generator chip has eight internal registers which control the three tone generators and their associated attenuators and the noise generator and its attenuator. Each byte of information sent to the sound generator chip contains a three-bit address used to select which register the information is destined for. The only complication is the frequency information for the tone generators. Obviously, to send a 10-bit number to a tone generator will need two bytes and hence two calls to the procedure PROCSOUND given above. The first byte contains the register address and four bits of the 10-bit number. The second byte carries the remaining six bits of

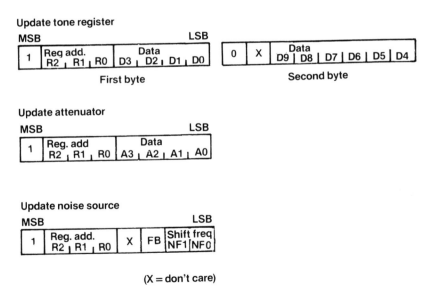

Fig. 5.5. Data formats for sound generator.

the number and is distinguished from all the others by having its most significant bit set to zero. The data formats used to write to each type of register can be seen in Figure 5.5. The appropriate register address bits select the register as follows:

R2	R1	R0	Register
0	0	0	Tone 1 frequency.
0	0	1	Tone 1 attenuation.
0	1	0	Tone 2 frequency.
0	1	1	Tone 2 attenuation.
1	0	0	Tone 3 frequency.
1	0	1	Tone 3 attenuation.
1	1	0	Noise control.
1	1	1	Noise attenuation.

If an attenuation register is selected then the format of the attenuation bits is:

A3	A2	A1	A0	Attenuation
0	0	0	0	0dB
0	0	0	1	2dB
0	0	1	0	4dB
0	1	0	1	8dB
1	0	0	0	16dB
1	1	1	1	OFF

If the noise control register is selected, then, if FB=0, the result is periodic noise and, if FB=1, the result is white noise. The two bits NF0 and NF1 control the frequency of the shift register's clock as indicated below:

NF1	NF0	Shift rate
0	0	N/512
0	1	N/1024
1	0	N/2048
1	1	Tone generator 3's output

As an example, consider the problem of using PROCSOUND to produce a white noise at full volume. This implies sending two bytes to the sound generator – the first setting the noise attenuator to 0dB and the second setting the noise control register to white noise. Thus the format of the first byte is 11110000. The first 1 is always present before a register address, the next three bits form the register address and the last four bits form the desired attenuation. Changing this to hex gives &F0 as the first byte to be sent using PROCSOUND. By similar reasoning the second byte works out to 11100100 or &E4. Thus the final program is:

```
10 PROCSOUND(&F0)
20 PROCSOUND(&E4)
30 STOP
```

(To which should be added PROCSOUND, of course.) As a final example, consider the following program:

```
10 PROCSOUND(&90)
20 PROCSOUND(&80)
30 PROCSOUND(RND AND &DF)
40 GOTO 30
```

The first byte sets the attenuation on tone generator 1 to 0dB. The second byte sets the first four bits of the 10-bit number sent to tone generator 1 to zero. The third byte sent by line 30 supplies the final six bits of the number at random. (RND AND &DF) generates a six-bit number. Lines 30 and 40 form a loop that repeatedly sends new random values for the six bits. It is a feature of the sound generator chip that any values that begin with zero will update the six bits of the last tone register selected. The result of this is that short random tones are generated until you press ESCAPE.

This description of the sound generator hardware within the BBC Micro should convince you how clever and convenient the SOUND and ENVELOPE commands are. For example, the sound generator chip has no facility for specifying the duration of a note. A note continues to sound until software turns it off using the attenuator setting. The BBC Micro uses the regular timer interrupt as an opportunity to see if the duration of a note specified in a SOUND command has been completed. If it has not the sound generator is left alone; if it has then the tone is switched off. By using interrupts in this way the BBC Micro can appear to be getting on with something else while the sound generator produces sounds! The action of the ENVELOPE command is also based on interrupts. Each envelope specifies a time unit after which the sound generator is updated. For example, if an envelope specifies a *step size* of one hundredth of a second then the attenuation and frequency of the selected tone generator is updated at each timer interrupt.

Conclusion

There is enough material concerning the BBC Micro's sound generator and sound generating software for a book dealing with nothing else! In this brief introduction there should be sufficient information to suggest many interesting and enjoyable uses of this remarkable facility. Whether you are interested in making music or programming impressive sound effects you will find enough scope for experimentation.

Chapter Six
Interfacing

In the context of computing, the term *interfacing* is taken to mean connecting any type of external equipment – including printers, disc drives and tape recorders. In this chapter, however, the subject is restricted to considering the BBC Micro's A to D convertor and the user port. The presence of these two facilities within the BBC Micro make it suited for a wide range of 'serious' tasks such as controlling experiments and other machinery, and making measurements automatically. The BBC Micro is ideally suited for this sort of application; its graphics capabilities can be put to good use displaying results or the current state of the equipment being controlled; the high speed calculating power of the BASIC can be used to process the measurements, and even the sound generator can be used to draw attention to an abnormal condition! This more serious side of the BBC Micro isn't entirely devoid of lighthearted applications. The A to D convertor can be used to connect a pair of joysticks or 'paddles' that bring a whole new dimension to playing games! Both the user interface and the A to D convertor are fitted only to the Model B machine.

In the first part of this chapter we consider the A to D convertor. This is a fairly straightforward device from the programmer's point of view in that the MOS and BASIC provide commands to handle the device and it is fairly easy to use even from assembly language. The difficulty with the A to D convertor lies in the electronics that you connect it to rather than the programs that you write afterwards. Unless you know a little about practical electronics, that is, can use a soldering iron and recognise a resistor from a diode, then you would be well-advised to connect only off-the-shelf extras such as the games paddles made by Acorn to the A to D convertor. The same is true for the user port, which also presents another level of difficulty in that the VIA which provides the user port is a very complex device. And to make matters worse, the BASIC and the

MOS provide nothing to control it. However, the effort spent in mastering it is certainly well worth it because it is extremely versatile.

The A to D convertor

Most of the things that we measure are *analog* in the sense that the results of the measurements range over a scale that is for all practical purposes continuous. Another way of thinking about this is to imagine the graph of the measurement with time. The graph of an analog quantity would be free to wander up and down without any restrictions. By contrast, the graph of a *digital* quantity is restricted to a finite number of values and is, therefore, always subject to some limitation that causes it to progress in *jumps*. For example, the graph of the number of computers manufactured per month cannot go up by a fractional amount! Digital quantities are normally easy to measure using a computer. For example, in the case of the number of computers produced per month, all you would have to do is arrange for the computer to add one to a variable every time a computer was produced. The exact details of how the BBC Micro would be informed that another computer had been produced is part of the subject studied in the second half of this chapter – digital interfacing. Measuring anolog quantities using a computer is slightly more difficult and really requires a special piece of hardware called an A to D convertor (Analog to Digital convertor). This takes an electrical signal and turns it into a number that can be read by the computer. Of course, to use an A to D convertor to measure any quantity, it must be first converted to an electrical signal that is proportional to the quantity. A device that carries out such a conversion is called a *transducer*. For example, a photo cell, or a

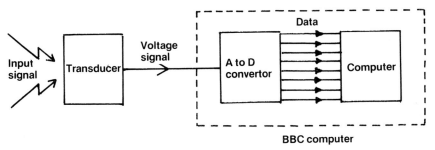

Fig. 6.1. Computer measuring system.

photo diode, is a transducer that converts light intensity to a voltage. Thus, a complete analog measuring system consists of three components – the computer, an A to D convertor and a transducer (see Figure 6.1). As the BBC Micro (Model B) comes equipped with an A to D convertor you can guess that most of our problems lie in the transducer. However, before considering transducers it is necessary to look at the capabilities and limitations of the BBC Micro's A to D convertor.

The A to D convertor used in the BBC Micro (a μPD7002) is a four channel 12-bit convertor. This means that it can select any one of four inputs to convert. However, it is important to notice that it can be engaged in converting only one of the four inputs at any one time! The '12-bit' part of the specification tells us how accurately the conversion is carried out. A 12-bit number lies in the range 0 to 4095 and this indicates how finely the A to D convertor divides up its input range. If the largest voltage that can be input to the A to D is Vmax then it is not difficult to see that the entire input range is divided into 4095 parts. This means that the smallest voltage change that can be detected is Vmax/4095 or roughly .02% of the maximum reading. When you compare this to the normal accuracy of 3% of maximum reading of conventional 'moving needle' meters you will realise that 12 bits of accuracy is very acceptable. Unfortunately, you cannot suppose that just because the A to D convertor returns results accurate to 12 bits that all of them reflect the quantity being measured. Allowing for noise etc., 10 bits of accuracy is all you can expect unless you take special care. Even so, 10 bits gives a range of 0 to 1024 which is an accuracy of roughly .1% of the maximum reading. This is still very good.

Apart from the number of channels and their accuracy, A to D convertors also differ in how fast they can produce a result. The A to D convertor in the BBC Micro takes 10 ms per conversion. This is not very fast and limits the sort of application that the BBC Micro can be used for. If an input signal varies during this conversion time the final result will not adequately reflect the input signal. In other words, any important variations in the signal must occur over a time that is roughly twice as long as the conversion time. (To be precise a signal can only be digitised accurately by the BBC Micro if its highest frequency component is less than 50 Hz.) If all four channels are in use then the situation is even worse. As each channel takes 10 ms for a conversion and each channel is treated in turn, any one channel is read only once every 40 ms. Although the speed on conversion limits the range of signals that can be converted accurately, it is perfectly fast enough for joystick signals, position measurement, temperature measurement etc.

A to D software

There are three commands that can be used to control the operation of the A to D convertor, ADVAL, *FX 16 and *FX 17. ADVAL is a BASIC function that can be used to find out the last reading from any of the A to D channels. For example:

X=ADVAL(2)

will store the most recent result from channel 2 (the channels are numbered from 1 to 4) in the variable X. The value that ADVAL actually returns is in fact the A to D value multiplied by 16. The reason for this strange action is that it allows for future improvement in A to D convertors to 16 bits accuracy. Thus the value returned by ADVAL varies over the range 0 to 65520 and changes in steps of 16. The reason why ADVAL returns the most recent value rather than the current value from the channel concerned is that in normal operation the A to D convertor is continually converting each channel in turn. At the end of each 10 ms conversion period the result is stored in memory ready for later use. Thus, whenever the ADVAL function is used it is the last value stored in memory that is returned as the result. This is a very sensible arrangement as it saves having to wait for the requested channel to have its turn in the sequence of conversion but it is as well to be aware of the fact that the value returned can be as much as 40 ms old. If you are using less than four channels then, obviously, converting all four in turn could be a waste of much-needed time. The MOS command *FX 16 can be used to remove any of the channels from the sequence of conversion.

   *FX 16,0 no channel is converted
   *FX 16,1 only channel 1 is converted
   *FX 16,2 channels 1 and 2 are converted alternately
   *FX 16,3 channels 1,2 and 3 are converted in turn
   *FX 16,4 each channel is converted in turn

Notice, that if you want to cut down the number of channels involved in conversion you must use the lower numbered channels first. If you want an up-to-date reading from any channel then you can use *FX 17, 'channel number' which will start a conversion on the channel corresponding to 'channel number'. Of course, following this command you will have to wait for 10 ms until the conversion is complete but it is the only way to get a completely up-to-date measurement. The function ADVAL (or the MOS OSBYTE call with A=&80 which is equivalent) can be used to find out when a channel has completed conversion. ADVAL(0) DIV 256 will give the number of the last channel to complete conversion. If no channel has completed conversion, then 0 is returned. So, if you initiate conversion on a particular channel, you should wait until its number is returned by ADVAL(0) 256. To see this in action try:

```
10 *FX 17,1
20 PRINT ADVAL(0) DIV 256
30 GOTO 20
```

You should see two zeros printed by line 20 indicating that channel 1 is still converting and then the sequence 1,2,3,4 over and over again as the normal sequence of conversion carries on.

This is all there is to the software to control the A to D convertor. Even from machine code it is simpler to use the OSBYTE equivalent of ADVAL, *FX 16 and *FX 17 rather than try to write your own subroutines. However, the ADVAL function does a little more than just deal with the A to D convertor. There are two *fire button* inputs provided on the analog input connector at the back of the BBC Micro and, as these are intended to be used with joysticks, they are also handled by the ADVAL function. The fire button inputs are digital inputs and so would be better described in the second half of this chapter. However, as they are handled by ADVAL it is worth saying that they can be used to detect whether or not a switch (usually a push button) is open or closed. The switch should be connected between the fire button input and a 0 V line provided on the same connector. (See the next section for more hardware information.) The state of the switches can be read by using:

X=ADVAL(0) AND 3

which returns a number with the following meaning:

X=0 no switch closed
1 left switch closed
2 right switch closed
3 both switches closed

The other uses of ADVAL (i.e. with a negative parameter) are very useful but have nothing to do with the A to D convertor.

Hardware for the A to D convertor

So far the discussion has been about using the A to D convertor from the software point of view. Before you can get to this stage, however, you have to have solved the problem of connecting a suitable transducer to the channel of your choice. The easiest way to do this is to buy an off-the-shelf transducer such as a pair of joysticks from Acorn. If you want to try something a little more adventurous then it is not difficult to connect your own transducers. The only thing that you need to know is that the voltage input to the A to D convertor must lie in the range 0 to 1.8 V. It is very important to keep within these limits because the A to D convertor chip itself is very easily damaged by input voltages outside this range. This warning sounds a little frightening but there is an output available from the analog connector – Vref (pins 11 and 14) – which is 1.8 V and if you use this to supply any transducers that you are using then you cannot possibly exceed the maximum input voltage. The voltage Vref is used by the A to D convertor as a *calibration* voltage. In other words, an input equal to Vref will give the maximum reading from the A to D convertor. Thus, to change the reading of the A to D into Volts, you need to measure the actual value of Vref (using a meter) accurately. Once you know Vref then the reading in volts is given by:

Volts=ADVAL(N)*Vref/65520

It is important to notice the accuracy of the A to D convertor depends on the accuracy and stability of Vref – which is not very good. If you are trying to make accurate measurement then it is better to connect a good calibration voltage to one of the channels and compare the reading on all the other channels with it.

The most simple and most common transducer is a variable resistor (potentiometer) used to convert the position of its spindle to a voltage. This is the principle behind most joysticks and paddles. You can see the circuit for a joystick or games paddle in Figure 6.2. The potentiometers are connected between Vref and analog ground. The voltage from the slider depends on its position and this is fed to the A to D convertor input. (10K potentiometers are used because they are large enough not to take too much current from Vref and yet small enough not to be affected by the connection of the A to D convertor input, which has an input impedance of approximately 10 MΩ.) The small capacitors are simply to remove any spurious signals and their exact value is unimportant. To make a pair of joysticks you would have to make up two copies of the circuit and

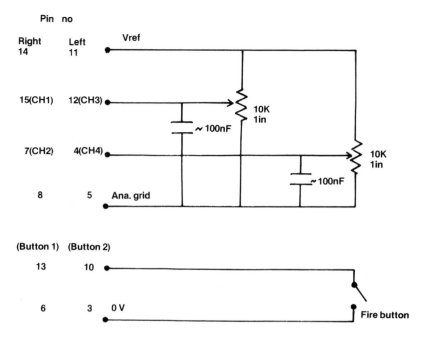

Fig. 6.2. Games paddles.

connect the first to the analog input pin numbers shown under the heading 'right' and the other to the pin numbers listed under 'left'.

The major problem encountered when connecting transducers to an A to D convertor is getting the voltage range of the output of the transducer into the range that the A to D convertor requires. The problem of reducing a larger range of voltages is easily solved using a voltage divider (Figure 6.3). If the maximum voltage input is Vin

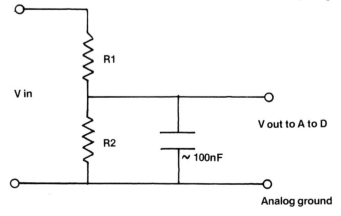

Fig. 6.3. A voltage divider.

then the maximum voltage output (Vout) to the A to D is given by:

Vout=R2*Vin/(R1+R2)

Obviously, R1 and R2 should be chosen to keep the maximum input voltage to the A to D lower than Vref to avoid any damage. Also, the value of R1+R2 should be kept large to avoid taking too much current from the transducer. The definition of too much depends on the transducer, of course, but R1+R2 should be large compared to the output impedance of the transducer to avoid distortion. The opposite problem of increasing the size of small signals can be solved only by the use of an amplifier, a topic which is beyond the scope of this book. For more information, see any book on practical operational amplifiers.

There are so many light sensors, either light sensitive diodes, transistors or resistors (including ones capable of detecting infra red), that it is impossible to recommend any particular one for experimental purposes. You should, however, have no trouble finding one to suit your application. Other sensors that might prove interesting are the FGS7712 flammable gas detector, the RS304-431 liquid flow sensor and the 590KH temperature sensor (all available from RS Components Ltd.).

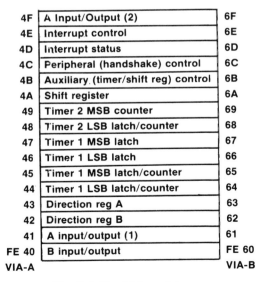

Fig. 6.4. The VIA registers.

The user interface and the 6522 VIA

As explained in Chapter One, there are two 6522 VIAs inside the BBC Micro Model B. VIA-A is used for internal functions apart from the two fire button inputs on the analog connector. VIA-B is only fitted to the Model B. It provides the parallel printer interface and the user port. The 6522 VIA is a complex device that is controlled by a set of sixteen different registers (Figure 6.4). Instead of dealing with each register in turn it makes more sense to describe the three basic functions of the VIA – input/output, timing and the shift register – and give BASIC procedures to control each. If more speed is required in any application then the procedures are easy to convert into assembly language subroutines. For reference purposes, the pin connections for the user port are given below:

Table 6.1. Pin connections for the user port connector.

Pin	Function	Pin	Function
1	+5 V	2	CB1
3	+5 V	4	CB2
5	ground	6	PB0
7	. .	8	PB1
9	. .	10	PB2
11	. .	12	PB3
13	. .	14	PB4
15	. .	16	PB6
17	ground	18	PB7

Input/output lines

Every VIA has twenty input/output lines grouped into an A side and a B side of ten lines each. These ten lines are further divided into a group of eight data lines and two special *handshake* lines. Most of the complications lie in the use of the handshake lines so consideration of these is left until later. The eight data lines are called PA0 to PA7 on the A side of the port and PB0 to PB7 on the B side. In principle, any of the data lines can be set to an input or an output line using the appropriate data direction register (registers 2 and 3). However, the BBC Micro uses the A side of VIA-B as a buffered output to drive the printer port so only the B side data lines can be used as inputs. To use a line as an output you have to store a one in the correct place in the appropriate data direction register. For example, to use PB3 as an output you must store a one in the b3 (bit 3) of the B data direction register. If you want to use a line as an output then you must store a zero in the same place. For example, the command ?&FE62=&F0 would set up PB0 to PB3 as inputs and PB4 to PB7 as outputs. The lines PA0 to PA7 are set up as outputs automatically by the MOS when the machine is switched on. The following BASIC procedure can be used to set any of the B side lines to outputs or inputs as desired.

```
100 DEF PROCIOSET(S$)
110 LOCAL I,S%
120 S%=0
130 FOR I=1 TO LEN(S$)
140 S%=S%+2^EVAL(MID$(S$,I,1))
150 NEXT I
160 ?&FE62=S%
170 ENDPROC
```

To set a line to an output, simply include its number in the string S$. For example, to set lines 3,5 and 7 to outputs, use PROCIOSET("357"). Lines 0,1,2,4 and 6 will be set to inputs by default.

The state of the output lines is controlled by writing to the A or B input/output registers. An output line can either by high i.e. 5 V, or low i.e. 0 V, and these states correspond to writing one and zero respectively to the same number bit in the input/output register. For example, ?&FE60=&01 sets PB0 high and PB1 to PB7 low, because the assignment sets bit 0 of the B input/output register to one and all the other bits to zero. This method of controlling output lines is not too difficult to use but it would be easier to have a command that would set a particular line high or low without affecting any of the others. The following two BASIC procedures do just this:

```
200 DEF PROCON(N%)
210 IF N%<0 OR N%>7 THEN ENDPROC
220 N%=2^N%
230 ?&FE60=?&FE60 OR N%
240 ENDPROC

300 DEF PROCOFF(N%)
310 IF N%<0 OR N%>7 THEN ENDPROC
320 N%=2^N%
330 ?&FE60=?&FE60 AND (NOT N%)
340 ENDPROC
```

The procedure PROCON will turn any line on, i.e. high, without affecting the state of any other line. For example, PROCON(5) will set line 5 high and leave everything else as it was. PROCOFF does the opposite and sets the selected line low, again without affecting any of the other lines. The only lines in the above procedures that might need any explanation are lines 230 and 330. You will notice that the address of the input/output register occurs on both sides of the expression. This is because you can not only write to the input/output register, you can also read it to discover what the output lines are currently set to.

Using lines set to inputs is just as easy. If you read from the input/output register then the current state of any input line is reflected in the state of the bits with the same number. If the input line is high i.e. set to 5 V, then the bit will be set to one and if the line is low then the bit will be set to zero. For example, if line PB2 is set to input and it has 5 V applied to it, then bit 2 in the input/output register is a one. The only problem is what happens if the voltage on the input line is between 0 V and 5 V. The answer is that the corresponding bit may or may not be set depending on the exact value of the voltage on the line. In general, reading the input/output register is unreliable if the input lines are not either at 0 V or 5 V. If you have some lines set to output and some set to input then you can write to the input/output register without fear of affecting the input line and you can read the input/output register to obtain the current state of the output and input lines. The function FNIN(N%) will return the state, zero or one of any line PB0 to PB7 irrespective of the line being an input or an output.

```
400 DEF FNIN(N%)
410 LOCAL S%
420 IF N%<0 or N%>7 THEN =-1
430 S%=?&FE60
440 S%=(S% DIV 2^N%) AND &01
450 =S%
```

For example, FNIN(3) returns the state, zero or one of line PB3.

This completes the discussion of using the data lines PB0 to PB7 as inputs or outputs. The data lines PA0 to PA7 are permanently set as outputs to the printer port but this doesn't mean that you cannot use them as extra output lines to supplement the user port. Any of the procedures or functions given above can be rewritten to use the A input/output register. Finally, it is worth pointing out that the output lines cannot be used to provide very much in the way of power to control things. You will almost certainly have to use a

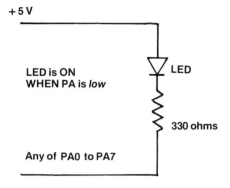

+5 V

LED is ON
WHEN PA is *low*

LED

330 ohms

Any of PA0 to PA7

Fig. 6.5. LED output.

transistor or a reed relay to switch any real equipment on and off. The 6522 can only sink 1.5 mA of current and provide about .5 mA and this is very little. However, you can drive an LED directly from the printer port, as shown in Figure 6.5, and this can be very useful while you are testing software or just learning about the user port. Similarly, Figure 6.6 shows a simple input circuit using a switch.

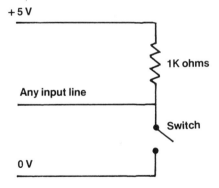

+5 V

1K ohms

Any input line

Switch

0 V

Fig. 6.6. Simple switch input.

The handshake lines

As mentioned in the previous section, there are two additional lines on the VIA. On the A side these are called CA1 and CA2 and on the B side they are called CB1 and CB2. Once again the A side lines are involved in the printer interface. However, CB1 and CB2 are available for use by the user and are brought out on the user port connector. CA1 and CB1 are both inputs and CA2 and CB2 can be set as either inputs or outputs. There are so many ways that the handshake lines can be used that it is only possible to give a summary here. In practice, the handshake lines are only required for applications where the BBC Micro is being connected to another computer or a piece of equipment that is as complicated as a computer. For simple applications the handshake lines are best ignored.

The handshake lines are controlled by the peripheral control register. Which bits of the register control which handshake line can be seen in Figure 6.7. The CA1 and CB1 inputs can each set bits in

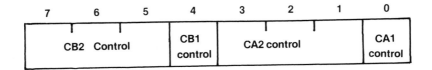

Fig. 6.7. The peripheral control register.

another VIA register – the interrupt status register. The corresponding CA1 and CB1 control bits govern when the bits are set. If the control bit is set to zero then the bit in the interrupt status register will be set to one when the voltage on the input line goes from high to low. If the control bit is a one then the bit in the interrupt status register is set when the voltage on the input line goes from low to high. Notice that this is different from the data lines in that the condition which sets the bit isn't a voltage level but a *change* in voltage levels. Such inputs are known as *edge triggered inputs*. Notice also that there is no mention of how the bits in the interrupt status register are set back to zero. This will be discussed in connection with the interrupt status register.

The CA2 and CB2 control bits have the following effects:

Table 6.2. Effects of CA2 and CB2 control bits.

Bits	*Effect*
3 2 1 (CA2) 7 6 5 (CB2)	
0 0 0	Input mode – set CA/B interrupt flag on negative transition of the input signal. The interrupt flag is cleared by a read or a write of the A/B input/output register respectively.

0 0 1	Input mode – set CA/B interrupt flag on negative transition of the input signal. The flag is *not* cleared by reading or writing the input/output register. The flag can only be cleared by writing a one to the interrupt status register (see later).
0 1 0	Input mode – as for 0,0,0 but flag set on positive transition of input signal.
0 1 1	Input mode – as for 0,1,0 but flag set on positive transition of input signal.
1 0 0	Output mode – CA/B 2 is set high by an active transition of CA/B 1 input. Reset by reading or writing A/B input/output register.
1 0 1	Output mode – CA/B 2 goes low for one cycle (of the 1 MHz clock) following a read or a write of the A/B input/output register.
1 1 0	Output mode – CA/B 2 always low.
1 1 1	Output mode – CA/B 2 always high.

The Timers

The 6522 VIA contains two timers. This sounds a little like over-provision – with two VIAs the Model B machine has four different timers at its disposal. However, each of the timers within a VIA has a different set of features designed to suit it to a particular application. Because of this difference between the timers it is worth dealing with them in turn. Both timers are controlled by bits within the *auxiliary control register* (see Figure 6.8).

Timer 1 consists of two main components. A sixteen bit latch and a sixteen bit counter. The latch is used to store a number that can be loaded into the counter which is continuously being decremented at

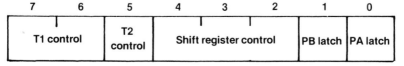

7	6	5	4	3	2	1	0
T1 control		T2 control	Shift register control			PB latch	PA latch

Fig. 6.8. The auxiliary control register.

the system clock rate i.e. 1 MHz. The latches can be written to and read directly at addresses &FE66 and &FE67 (on VIA-B). However, they are also used whenever the counter is loaded at addresses &FE64 and &FE65. If the low order byte of the counter was loaded directly then its value would have changed by the time the high order byte was loaded (remember the counter is continuously decrementing). To get round this problem, data that is written to the low order byte of the counter is in fact stored in the low order byte of the latch. Writing data to the high order byte of the counter not only loads the high order byte of the latch as a side effect but also causes the low order byte of the latch to be loaded into the low order byte of the counter. Using this method, the high and low order bytes of the counter are loaded at the same time. The latch holds any value stored in it until it is changed.

Timer 1 has two distinct operating modes – *single shot* and *free running*. In addition, it can also cause an output on PB7 every time the counter reaches zero. The function of the bits in the auxiliary control register are as shown below:

Table 6.3. Timer 1 control bits.

Bits 7 6	Effect
0 0	Set the T1 interrupt flag after the counter has reached zero after being loaded (single shot mode).
0 1	Set T1 interrupt flag after the counter has reached zero after having been loaded. Automatically reload the counter from the latch each time it reaches zero (free running mode).
1 0	Single shot mode but PB7 goes low when the high order counter/latch is loaded and returns high after when the T1 interrupt flag is set.
1 1	Free running mode but the output of PB7 is inverted each time the T1 interrupt flag is set.

The best way to explain the working of the two modes is by example. If we want to wait for a fixed time interval in a program then we need to use T1 in its single shot mode. After setting the appropriate bits in the auxiliary register to place T1 in single shot mode, the low order byte of the count is loaded into the latch/counter at &FE64. To start the countdown for the time interval all you have to do is load the high order byte of the count into the latch/counter at &FE65. To detect the end of the time interval, i.e. when the counter reaches zero, you can either examine bit 6 in the interrupt status register at &FE6D until it becomes 1 or you can enable the T1 interrupt and write an interrupt service routine (as described in Chapter Three). To repeat the time interval, all you have to do is load the high byte latch/counter. The number that has to be loaded into the counter to produce any given time interval is easy to determine. If the counter is loaded with n then the flag will be set after $n+1.5$ μs. If the PB7 output is enabled, then you will also get a single pulse out of the PB7 line lasting for the same time interval. When the counter reaches zero it continues to decrement so the counter registers can be used by the processor to find out how long ago the counter reached zero.

The free running mode is very similar to the single shot mode except for the fact that the counter, both high and low order bytes, are reloaded from the latch each time the counter reaches zero. This allows a series of interrupts and, if the output of PB7 is enabled, a series of pulses to be produced. You can change the values stored in the latches by writing to the latch registers at &FE66 and &FE67 while the count is being decremented. The new value will be loaded into the counter the next time it reaches zero. Using this method you can produce pulses of varying length in a continuous stream.

Timer 2 operates as a timer in the single shot mode only and as a counter. As a timer it is more limited than timer 1, not only because it cannot be used in a free running mode, but because there is no way of reading or writing to the latches directly. Setting timer 2's counters follows the same pattern as for timer 1 in single shot mode. First the low order byte is loaded into the low order latch at &FE68, then the high order byte is loaded into the counter at &FE69 which also transfers the contents of the low order latch into the low order counter. The counter then decrements until it reaches zero when it sets the T2 interrupt flag in the interrupt status register. No output pulse can be produced with timer 2. The second mode in which timer 2 can be operated is a pulse-counting mode. In this mode a number can be loaded into the counter registers in the same way as in single shot mode. However, the counter now decrements each time a (negative going) pulse is applied to PB6. The T2 interrupt flag is set when the counter reaches zero but the counter still decrements with each input pulse. The T2 control bit (bit 5 in the auxiliary control register) selects the operating mode of timer 2. If it is zero then the timer operates in a single shot mode. If it is one then the timer operates as a counter.

As a practical example of using the timers requires assembly language, it is postponed until Chapter Eight.

The shift register

The 6522 VIA contains an eight bit *re-cycling shift register*. It can be used either in an input or output mode. In an input mode bits are *shifted* into the register from CB2. In an output mode, bits are shifted out to the same CB2 line. Apart from this choice of input or output mode the only other variation in the way that the shift register works is the selection of the source or speed of the clock that causes a bit to be shifted into or out of the register. When the shift clock is derived internally it is available on the CB1 line and when it is derived externally it is supplied though CB1. The shift register's operating mode is controlled by bits 2 to 4 in the auxiliary control register as follows:

Table 6.4. Shift register control bits.

Bits 4 3 2	Effects
0 0 0	Shift register disabled.
0 0 1	Shift in controlled by timer 2.
0 1 0	Shift in controlled by system clock (1 MHz).
0 1 1	Shift in controlled by external pulses on CB1.
1 0 0	Free running output controlled by timer 2.
1 0 1	Shift out controlled by timer 2.
1 1 0	Shift out controlled by the system clock (1 MHz).
1 1 1	Shift out controlled by external pulses on CB1.

In each of the modes apart from the free running mode the shift out or in is initiated by writing or reading the shift register and after eight shift pulses the shift register interrupt flag is set to one in the interrupt register. If the shift clock is derived internally this stops after eight pulses. However, in the free running mode the shift clock is applied continuously. As the shift register recycles, the same eight bits are sent out over CB2 repeatedly.

The shift register is a fairly specialised device in that it is generally used to transfer information from one computer to another. However, the free-running mode can be used to generate short irregular pulse trains by loading the shift register with the correct pattern of ones and zeros.

The interrupt control and status register

While discussing the various functions of the VIA, the setting of a bit in the interrupt status register has often been used as a way of indicating that something has happened. In fact, the interrupt status register works as a pair with the interrupt control register (see Figure 6.9). The meaning of all of the bits in the interrupt status register has already been explained apart from bit 7 or IRQ. The 6522 VIA can cause an IRQ interrupt (see Chapter Three) if so desired when any selected bits in the interrupt status register are first set to one. Bit 7 is

7	6	5	4	3	2	1	0	
IRQ	T1	T2	CB1	CB2	SR	CA1	CA2	Interrupt flags
Set/ clear	T1	T2	CB1	CB2	SR	CA1	CA2	Interrupt control

Fig. 6.9. Interrupt status/control registers.

one if the VIA has caused an IRQ interrupt and zero otherwise. Whether the setting of a bit in the interrupt status register actually causes an interrupt or not depends on the setting of the corresponding bit in the interrupt control register. For example, if T2 is 1 in the interrupt control register then the VIA will cause an IRQ interrupt as soon as the T2 bit in the interrupt status register is set to one. The bits in the interrupt status register can be cleared either indirectly by the methods described in the previous sections (for example, bit T2 is cleared by reading the T2 low order counter) or directly by writing to the register with the corresponding bit set to one. For example, to clear bit 3, i.e. CB2, but leave all the others unaffected you would write &08 to the interrupt status register. Setting a bit to one or zero in the interrupt control register also uses an odd method. To alter a given bit you must write to the interrupt control register a value with a one in the same bit position. If bit 7 of the value is a 1 then the selected bit (or bits) will be set to one. If bit 7 of the value is a 0 then the selected bit (or bits) will be set to zero. In other words, the selected bits are set to the same state as bit 7. An interrupt flag that is not enabled will not cause an IRQ interrupt but can still be set and cleared in the same way as normal.

Data latching

There are two bits left in the auxiliary control register that haven't been discussed so far – the PB and PA latch bits. If either of these bits are set to one then the input data to the A and B sides will be latched when the CA1 and CB1 interrupt flags are set to one respectively. In this mode reading the input/output registers returns the data values most recently latched rather than the current state of the input lines. The advantage of this is that fast changing data can be held automatically for the processor to read at a later date.

Conclusion

This chapter began with a warning that the 6522 VIA was a complicated device. By the end of this chapter you should be convinced that it is indeed complicated but you should be beginning to see how versatile it really is – living up to its name of Versatile Interface Adaptor. The only way you can become familiar with any area of interfacing is to make use of the information in a practical problem. Using the BBC Micro's A to D convertor and its VIA is no exception to this rule.

Chapter Seven
Introduction to Assembly Language

There is no question that BASIC is easy to learn and easy to use. It is also good enough for most applications. However, it has one major drawback – it is slow. The way to get the maximum performance from any computer is to write programs in its own language – the machine's *assembly language*. Notice that it is *the machine's* assembly language, because it is important to realise that there isn't a single language called 'assembly language'. Each machine, or rather each microprocessor, has its very own language. The BBC Micro uses a 6502 microprocessor, so its assembly language is more properly called '6502 assembly language'.

There is no avoiding the fact that assembly language is more difficult to learn than BASIC. If this were not the case everyone would learn assembly language before BASIC! Even though assembler isn't as easy as BASIC it is very well worth knowing and the BBC Micro makes it as easy as possible by having a built-in assembler. Using this facility you can mix BASIC and assembler very easily. You can write most of any program in BASIC and use assembler whenever BASIC proves to be too slow. This is really the best of both worlds!

This is the first of two chapters dealing with assembly language on the BBC Micro. The main subject of this chapter is the 6502, its assembly language and the BBC Micro's assembler. The next chapter shows how our knowledge of assembler, together with an understanding of the hardware, can be used to advantage. You could say that this chapter aims to teach you assembler and the next aims to teach you how to use assembler!

What makes assembler different?

The statement that BASIC is slow and assembler is fast may have made you wonder why this is so? The main reason for this speed difference is that BASIC is not a language that the 6502 inside the BBC Micro can obey directly. As already mentioned, the only language that it can obey is 6502 assembly language. The execution of your BASIC program involves the use of another program, called an interpreter. When you type RUN, the interpreter (in ROM 0 – see Chapter One) looks at the first line of your program and carries out your instructions. For example, if your first line reads GOTO 1000 the interpreter first identifies the GOTO and as a result looks for line number 1000. Once it finds line number 1000 (which may involve examining a lot of line numbers) it 'looks' to see what the line tells it to do next. Notice that your BASIC program doesn't directly control what the machine is doing. It controls what the interpreter, an assembly language program, is doing and it is the interpreter that controls the action of the 6502 microprocessor. This is, of course, the reason why BASIC is slower than assembly code.

Assembly language is executed by the 6502 without any intervening programs. If you give an assembly language command such as JMP &2000 (JMP is short for JUMP and so the instruction reads jump to &2000) which is the assembly language equivalent of GOTO then the 6502 carries it out at once. Not only does it carry it out immediately, there is no searching for the specified line number because assembly language doesn't work in terms of line numbers. Whenever an assembly language instruction refers to a position in a program it uses memory addresses. Thus JMP &2000 means jump to (or go to) memory location &2000 (remember the & means that the number following is in hexadecimal) and carry out the instruction that you find stored there. This is an advantage in that the 6502 doesn't have to spend time searching for a line number. After all, memory location &2000 is always in the same place, but it does mean that assembly language programs can only be run in the area of memory that they are written for. When you write a BASIC program you make no reference as to where in memory it should 'live' – in fact, it is one of the good things about BASIC that the program's location is irrelevant. Whenever you write GOTO 2000 you don't need to worry about where line 2000 is – the BASIC interpreter looks after you! This use of memory locations typifies assembly language. If you want to store some information then you have to say where you want it stored. In BASIC you simply use a variable and let the interpreter decide where things are stored.

Inside the 6502

The range of instructions that you can give the 6502 in assembly language is very much more limited than the sort of things you can write in BASIC. In particular, you can only handle one memory location at a time. Things are even more restricted than this because before you can do anything to the contents of a memory location, it must be brought 'inside' the 6502. This idea is easier to understand once you know that there are a number of special places inside the 6502 called *registers* where the contents of a memory location can be stored. Registers are the places where all the work gets done. For example, if you want to add the contents of two memory locations together you first have to load a register with the contents of the first location and then issue a command that adds the contents of the second location to the contents of the register. If you want the answer stored in a third memory location then you have to add yet another instruction to store the contents of the register in the memory location. Notice that something that would have been one instruction in BASIC, such as LET A=B+C, has become three instructions in assembly language!

As most 6502 operations involve the use of at least one register it is important to know what registers the 6502 has. To this end a summary can be seen in Figure 7.1. These six registers A, X, Y, PC, S

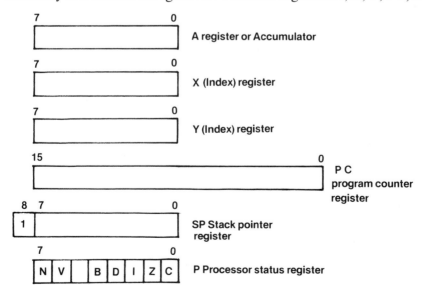

Fig. 7.1. The 6502 registers.

and P are the only registers that the 6502 has and part of the problem of assembly language programming is finding out how to do something useful with so few! As you might have guessed, each register has a different role to play. For example, the A register can be used to do things like arithmetic etc., while the X and Y registers are reserved for other duties. To become a good assembly language programmer you must know not only what registers are inside the 6502 but also what they can be used for.

The only register that need concern us for the moment is the A register. The A register is used for operations such as addition and subtraction. Surprisingly, it is the only register in the 6502 that can be used to carry out calculations of this sort. So if you want to do some arithmetic it is sure to involve the A register. For example, the small addition program that was introduced earlier involves the A register. Coded in 6502 assembly language it is:

```
LDA &2000
ADC &2001
STA &2002
```

The first instruction means 'LoaD A from memory location &2000'. The second instruction is 'ADd with Carry memory location &2001 to the A register' which, for the moment, can be taken to mean 'add the contents of memory location &2001 to the A register'. The final instruction is 'STore the A register in memory location &2002'. This is a complete assembly language program as long as we assume that the two numbers to be added together are already stored in memory locations &2000 and &2001 and the answer is actually needed in location &2002!

From assembly language to machine code

Although the example given at the end of the last section is a complete assembly language program it is not in a form that the 6502 can use. Humans find instructions written in the form LDA useful because it helps you to remember that the instruction means 'LoaD the A register'. However, as the 6502 cannot read letters, commands such as LDA have to be presented in the form of a numeric code. Every instruction that the 6502 obeys can be written in two ways – as a number and as a three-letter *mnemonic code*. The number form is for the 6502 and the letter form is easier for humans to deal with. For example, LDA is the mnemonic code for 'load the A register from a memory location' and its code is &AD. Before any assembly language program can be carried out by the 6502 it must be changed from mnemonic code form into a list of numbers – *machine code*. This could be done manually by looking up the machine code that corresponds to each mnemonic code in a table of such codes. However, looking that up in such a table, though simple, is such a time-consuming task that it is easier to get a program to do the conversion for us. Such a program is called an *assembler*.

The BBC assembler

The BBC Micro has within it a fairly standard 6502 assembler. This means that you can type in the mnemonic codes of assembly language and have the BBC Micro convert them to machine code. To see this try the following:

```
10 P%=&3000
20 [
30 LDA &2000
40 ADC &2001
50 STA &2002
60 ]
```

The '[' in line 20 indicates that what follows is assembler rather than BASIC. As you might guess, the matching ']' in line 60 marks the end of assembler and the start of more BASIC (if any). In general, the BBC Micro treats anything between square brackets as assembler. Lines 30 to 50 should be familiar as they formed the earlier example that added two numbers together. The only unexplained line is line 10. You will recognise P% as one of the *resident integer variables* discussed in Chapter Two. Just like a program in any language, an assembly language program needs to be stored somewhere in memory and the value of P% governs where. Setting P% to &3000 means that the first number that makes up the machine code of the program will be stored in location &3000. If you run the program you should see:

```
>RUN
3000
3000 AD 00 20 LDA &2000
3003 6D 01 20 ADC &2001
3006 8D 02 20 STA &2002
>
```

If you look at the first line of the display following the 3000 you can see AD which is the machine code for LDA. Following this the numbers 00 20 can be recognised as the address of the memory location that A is to be loaded from, but written in the wrong order! Each of the subsequent lines is in the same format i.e. 6D is the machine code for ADC and once again the address of the memory location follows but in the wrong order. The effect of setting P% to 3000 can also be seen in the column of numbers on the left-hand side. The first number in the machine code, AD is stored in memory location &3000, the second 00 is stored in &3001 and the third &20 in &3002 and so on to the end of the program. If you want to check that it is true type in (in immediate mode):

PRINT ~?&3000

which will print the contents of location &3000 in hexadecimal so that you can compare it with what you expect to be stored there. Try the same command with different addresses just to confirm that the program has been stored in the memory locations you expect.

It is important to be absolutely clear what has happened in the above program. The opening [told the machine that what followed was assembler and this caused the BBC Micro's assembler to convert the mnemonic codes to machine code and store the numbers in memory starting at the address stored in P%. The closing] switched the machine back to obeying BASIC statements. In this case there were no BASIC statements so the program stopped as you would expect. Notice that there is no mention of 'running' the assembly language program. All that has happened is that it has been converted to machine code and stored in memory starting at &3000. The result of this program can be summarised in terms of getting the assembly language ready to run somewhere in memory. Running the program is a separate step.

Making space

The BBC Micro's RAM is used for all sorts of things – temporary memory storage for the MOS, space for BASIC variables, video storage, and so on. To be able to store machine code safely we have to find an area of memory that isn't going to be used to store anything else afterwards. Storing machine code in areas of memory that are used for other purposes can be disastrous – you can lose control of the machine, the only cure for which is to switch the machine off and on. In the addition example in the last section, the area of memory starting at &3000 is used to store either lines of

BASIC or BASIC variables (see Chapter Two for more information). In this case, as the program is so small and doesn't use any variables it is a good bet that the &3000 area is unused. However, if the assembler language in the example was part of a larger program, progress would not be so easy. We obviously need some way of reserving an area of memory that can be used to store machine code. The standard way of reserving memory to store anything is to use a BASIC variable or a BASIC array. BBC BASIC provides a special sort of array, a *byte array*, that can be used to reserve memory for machine code. Try the following program:

```
10 DIM CODE% 10
20 P%=CODE%
30 [
40 LDA &2000
50 ADC &2001
60 STA &2002
70 ]
```

Line 10 is a special version of the DIM statement – notice that there are no brackets around the 10. It works in roughly the same way as a normal DIM statement in that it reserves storage in the variables area but there are two important differences. The statement DIM CODE% 10 reserves 11 memory locations and stores the address of the first memory location in the variable CODE%. In general the statement:

DIM numeric variable size

will reserve *size+1* memory locations and store the address of the first in *numeric variable*. The variable created by this statement can be used just like any other variable – it can be assigned to or used in arithmetic expressions. In particular, it can be used to set P% to the address of the reserved area of memory. This is exactly what is done in line 20. If you run the program you will see that the assembly language is changed to machine code as in the earlier example but now it is stored in the area of memory reserved by the DIM statement in line 10. The actual location of this area of memory will change as the size of the BASIC program that the assembly language is part of changes but the most important thing is that it will not change or be used for anything else after you type RUN.

There is another way of reserving memory for use by assembly language programs but this is a little more specialised and will be introduced later.

A running program

At this point we know how to use the BBC assembler to translate assembler to machine code and store it in an area of reserved memory. Unfortunately, before we can move onto an assembly language program that can be run we will have to abandon the addition example that has served us so well and write something a little more useful. The trouble with the addition example is that it added together two numbers that were already supposed to be stored in &2000 and &2001 and then stored the answer in &2002. This is not the best way to get information to and from a program! An interesting example is provided by a program that writes the letter 'A' on the screen – over and over again. In other words we will write the assembly language equivalent of:

```
10 PRINT "A";
20 GOTO 10
```

The first problem we have to solve is to find a way of writing something on the screen. We could use an assembly language version of the peek and poke graphics techniques introduced in Chapter Four but this would be very difficult and long-winded. Instead, we can make use of a subroutine in the MOS that writes characters on the screen. This subroutine is a machine code subroutine that is already in ROM so in this sense we are not cheating – our whole program is still machine code! A description of the subroutine can be found, along with other useful subroutines, in the User Guide. They are, however, worth repeating here.

The OSASCI (Operating System ASCII print) subroutine begins at memory location &FFE3. It will print the character whose ASCII code is stored in the A register on the screen at the cursor's current position and then move the cursor on one place.

To use this subroutine all we need to know is how to load the ASCII code of the character that we want to appear on the screen and also what the assembly language equivalent of GOSUB is. The first problem is solved by using the 6502's *immediate mode*. If you write LDA &02 this is taken to mean 'load the A register with the contents of memory location &0002'. However, if you write LDA &02 then this is taken to mean 'load the A register with the number 2'. In assembler a number should be taken to be the address of a memory location unless it is preceded by ' '. Using this information it should be easy for you to work out how to load the A register with the ASCII code for 'A'. The answer is LDA 65 (as 65 decimal is the ASCII code for A). The second problem is even easier to solve by using the JSR – Jump to SubRoutine – command, which is almost the exact assembly language equivalent of GOSUB except that it transfers control to an address rather than a line number. While we are on the subject, it is worth mentioning that the assembly language equivalent of RETURN is simply RTS – ReTurn from Subroutine.

We can now begin to write the program:

```
10 DIM CODE% 20
20 P%=CODE%
30 [
40   LDA #65
50   JSR &FFE3
60 ]
```

Lines 10 and 20 are familiar from the previous example. The size of the area reserved is set to 21 bytes which should be more than big enough for the machine code generated. Line 40 is the first line of the assembly language proper and this simply loads the A register with 65 (decimal). Line 50 is the jump to the operating system subroutine. This chunk of program will print the letter A on the screen once. What we want to do, however, is print the letter A repeatedly on the screen. The easiest way to do this is to add JMP (JuMP), the assembly language equivalent of GOTO, to the end of the program. To print the letter A repeatedly we want to JMP back to the instruction that jumps to the subroutine, namely the JSR instruction. The problem is how to specify this in the JMP instruction. If you recall the earlier discussion, assembly language instructions work with memory addresses so we need to know the address of the JSR instruction. This is something that we could find out by running the above program, noting the address at which the machine code equivalent of JSR is stored. Unfortunately, this won't do us any good because as soon as we add the JMP instruction to the program the area of memory where the program is stored moves, and with it the location of the JSR instruction!

The solution to this problem lies in the use of *labels*. A label is a standard BASIC variable that is used to store the address of a memory location. So, for example, CODE% is a label which indicates the start of the reserved area of memory. You can define a label within an assembly language program by writing a full stop and then its name. The label then stores the address that the next instruction will be stored in. Once defined, you can use a label anywhere that you can use an address. Putting these two pieces of information together we can write the program as:

```
10 DIM CODE% 20
20 P%=CODE%
30 [
40        LDA #65
50 .LOOP JSR &FFE3
60        JMP LOOP
70 ]
```

Line 50 now defines the label 'LOOP' as the address of the JSR instruction and Line 60 can be read as 'JuMP to LOOP' and will transfer control to the JSR instruction no matter what address it is actually at. To prove that labels are really just BASIC variables try PRINT LOOP after running the program – the number that is printed is the address of the JSR instruction.

Now we have a complete program, the only thing left to do is to run the machine code that results from the assembler. To do this we need to use one of two BASIC statements that transfer control to machine code, USR and CALL.

The easiest to use in this situation is CALL 'address' which will transfer control to the machine code instruction stored at 'address'. If you add:

80 CALL CODE%

and run the program you will at last see the screen fill with letter As! If you try to stop the program you will find that the ESCAPE key has no effect and the only way that you can stop the program is to press BREAK. You shouldn't worry. This is simply a reflection of the fact that machine code isn't as easy to control as BASIC! (You can type OLD to get the program back.)

Addressing modes

Now we have written a working program all that remains to do is expand our knowledge of 6502 instructions. Roughly speaking there are two parts to every instruction – one that gives information about what to do and another that gives information about what to do it to. For example, in LDA &2000, the LDA is what to do and the &2000 is where to do it from. Technically, the ways in which you can specify where to carry out an operation are referred to as *addressing modes*. It is easier to learn the range of addressing modes that the 6502 has and then look at what instructions can be used with what addressing modes rather than to treat everything as a special case. On first reading don't try to remember all the addressing modes, just familiarise yourself with their names and the ideas involved. Like most things, addressing modes are easier to understand and remember when you actually need to use them.

Absolute addressing

This is the simplest and most used method of addressing. The address of the memory location that contains the data to be operated on is written following the operation code. For example, LDA &2000 or STA DATA (where DATA is a label).

Zero page addressing

This is a special case of absolute addressing that is used when the address is in the range 0 to 255. Zero page memory locations are special because their addresses can be held in a register or a single memory location. This is because the range 0 to 255 can be represented using only eight bits. However, the address of any other memory location cannot be held in a register and has to be stored using two memory locations because it requires sixteen bits to represent it. There are a number of other addressing modes that only work with the 'help' of page zero memory locations – for example, LDA $05.

Immediate addressing

In this form of addressing, the value to be operated on is written, preceded by , after the operation code. For example, LDA 20 loads the value 20 into the A register; LDA DATA loads the value of the label DATA into the A register.

Accumulator and implied addressing

Sometimes an instruction can be applied to either a memory location or to the accumulator. To show that the accumulator is the subject of the operation you must write 'A' where an address would normally go. This is known as *accumulator addressing*. In other cases the place where the operation is to be carried out is implied in the instruction. For example, there is no address specified in RTS. This is known as *implied addressing*. Neither are very common nor particularly difficult to understand when they occur.

Relative addressing

This form of addressing tends to look like absolute addressing from the user's point of view. If you are at a particular point in a program you could specify a memory location by saying how many locations above or below the current location it is. This is known as *relative addressing*. The only instructions that use relative addressing are the 'branch' instructions, and the BBC assembler automatically converts absolute addresses to relative when used with branch instructions.

Indexed addressing

This is the most complicated and versatile form of addressing that we have looked at so far. It also involves two registers that we haven't used until now – the X and Y registers. An example of an instruction using indexed addressing is LDA &2312,X. The address that the A register is loaded from is given by adding the contents of the X register to the absolute address on the left of the comma. For example, if X contained &50, then A would be loaded from &2321+&50 or &2371. In general, the address used in indexed addressing is obtained by adding the absolute (or zero page) address to the left of the comma to the contents of the register (X or Y) to the right – for example, LDA 34,X, STA DATA, Y etc.

The main use for indexing is in 'scanning' through a table of values. The absolute address is the start of the table and the index register is set to the *offset*, that is the distance from the start of the table that you wish to examine. Moving through the table is carried out using INX (INcrement X), INY (INcrement Y), DEX (DEcrement X), and DEY (DEcrement Y).

Indirect addressing

This is a form of addressing that often confuses beginners. However, there is nothing complicated about it. Indirect addressing is usually denoted by enclosing an address in brackets, e.g. (&2320) is an indirect address. The location that an indirect address refers to isn't the location that finally interests us; instead, it contains the *address* of the location that interests us. For example, (&2320) refers to the memory location &2320 the contents of which are then used as the address of the memory location that will be used in the operation. You can use indirection brackets around any other type of addressing or indeed any part of any type of addressing. For example, (&34,X) is an instruction using indexed indirect addressing. To work out the memory location it refers to, you have to work out the address within the brackets and then use the contents of this memory location as the address of the memory location that the instruction refers to. (It is a restriction of the 6502 that this sort of indirect addressing only works if the address in the brackets is a zero page address, i.e. is in the range 0 to 255.)

There are restrictions on the way you can use indirection with the 6502. In particular there are only three ways that indirection brackets can be combined with other addressing modes.

1. *Absolute indirect*. This is the basic form of indirection where an absolute address is enclosed in an indirection bracket. The final address is simply the contents of the memory location whose address is between the brackets. There is one complication in that two memory locations are involved in absolute indirection, the one referred to by the absolute address and the next highest. This is because two memory locations are required to hold an address. There is also one major restriction in that absolute indirect addressing can only be used with one 6502 instruction – JMP. Thus JMP (&1234) takes the contents of memory locations &1234 and &1235 and treats them as the address to jump to.

2. *Indexed indirect addressing*. This form of indirect addressing only works using the X register and is written (&32,X). The final address is worked out by adding the zero page absolute address to the contents of the X register and then using the result as the address of a page zero memory location. This page zero memory location together with the one above it hold the address of the memory location that the instruction will use. For example, LDA (&32,X) first adds 32 to the contents of the X register. The resulting number is then used as a zero page address which, together with the next highest memory location, contains the absolute address of the memory location the A register is loaded from.

3. *Indirect indexed addressing*. This form of indirection is written (&23),Y and can only be used with the Y register. The final address is obtained by using the contents of the zero page address in brackets together with the next higher location as the address that is added to the contents of the Y register. For example, STA (&43),Y takes the contents of locations 43 and 44 and adds the resulting number to the contents of Y to form the address of the location that A is stored in.

You may be puzzled as to what some of the above addressing modes are used for. Don't worry too much because when you need to use an addressing mode its purpose will become clear! The only addressing modes that you need to understand at this point are: absolute, immediate and indexed.

The 6502's registers

The A register is by now familiar to us from earlier examples and the X and Y registers were introduced in the section above. We therefore already know something about three of the 6502's registers. However, this still leaves the PC, SP and P registers unexplained. For reference purposes, descriptions of each register in turn are given below.

The A register
This register is used for nearly all *data manipulation* – for example, addition and subtraction. It is the register that does most of the work in a program.

The X and Y registers
These registers are called *index registers* because of the role they play in indexed addressing. A good way of thinking about this is that the A register is used for handling data and the X and Y registers are concerned with addresses. However, this is not the whole truth because the X and Y registers can both be loaded from and stored in memory and this sometimes makes them useful for holding temporary results and moving data about when the A register is otherwise occupied. Notice that the X and Y registers are not entirely identical; there are some instructions that can use only the X register for index addressing.

The PC register
The PC or Program Counter register is almost an internal register that is used by the 6502 itself, in that there are no instructions that explicitly make use of the PC register. It used to hold the address of the current machine code instruction, that is, the one that the 6502 is obeying. The only instructions which modify the PC register are things like JMP &3432, which causes the PC register to be loaded with &3432 which then, of course, becomes the address of the next instruction to be carried out. It is not very often that a programmer needs to think about the PC register – it takes care of itself.

The SP register
The SP or Stack Pointer is another of the 6502's registers that the programmer needn't worry about too much. The SP register holds an address in a region of memory from 256 to 511. This region is

known as the *stack*, hence the name *stack pointer*. There are only two operations that can be applied to the SP register – push and pull. The SP starts with the address of the top of the stack, i.e. 511. A push instruction stores data on the stack at the address that the SP is 'pointing' at and then subtracts one from the SP register so that it is still pointing to an unused memory location. A pull instruction works the opposite way from a push instruction in that it adds one to the SP register and then retrieves data from the memory location that it is pointing at. These are the basic stack operations.

The 6502 itself uses the stack for temporary storage. For example, the JSR instruction stores the return address on the stack and the RTS instruction retrieves it from the stack. The stack can also be used for temporary storage in programs using instructions like PLA – PuLl A – which pulls data off the stack and stores it in A. However, unless you are absolutely sure what you are doing, the stack is best left alone.

The P register

The P or Condition register is different from all the other registers in that it is not used to hold either addresses or data. Instead, it stores information concerning the results of the last instruction executed and the machine in general. Each of the bits in the register can be thought of as *flags* that indicate a different condition. If you look again at Figure 7.1 you will see that each flag is given a single letter name. The B,D and I flags are concerned with the state of the machine. The B flag is 1 following a BRK instruction. The D flag sets the arithmetic mode of the 6502. When it is 0, arithmetic is done in binary and when it is 1 arithmetic is done in a form of decimal known as BCD – Binary Coded Decimal. The I flag is concerned with the servicing of interrupts. If it is a 1, then the 6502 cannot be interrupted. Interrupts are beyond the scope of this introduction to assembly language and my advice is to avoid their use! The flags that are most interesting to the programmer are the N,V,Z and C flags. These are set according to the result of the last instruction. For example, the N flag is 1 if the result of the last instruction was Negative. The V flag is a 1 if the result of the last operation was too big to be stored in a single memory location, i.e. it is the oVerflow flag. The Z flag is a 1 if the result of the last instruction was exactly Zero. Finally, the C flag is a 1 if there was a Carry from the last operation.

The main use of the P register is via the branch group of instructions. For example, suppose you want to transfer control somewhere but only when the contents of the A register are zero. This can be done by using BEQ, meaning 'Branch if EQual to zero', which tests the Z flag and jumps to the location only if it is equal to 1, i.e. if the result of the last instruction was zero. Thus the loop:

```
.LOOP DEX
      BEQ EXIT
      JMP LOOP
```

will come to an end when the X register contains zero. There is a simpler way to write this loop using the BNE 'Branch if Not Equal to zero' instruction:

```
.LOOP DEX
      BNE LOOP
```

which will keep on looping until the X register is zero. The P register used in conjunction with the branch instructions is the assembly language equivalent of the BASIC IF statement.

The 6502's instruction set

The only way to learn the instruction set of a microprocessor is to write the programs. However, it is necessary to have a rough idea of the sort of things a micro can do, so the full instruction set is listed with comments in Table 7.1.

Table 7.1.   The 6502 instruction set

Mnemonic code	Brief description	Addressing modes
ADC	Add memory to accumulator with carry.	IMM ABS ZPG (ABS,X) (ABS),Y ZPG,X ABS,X ABS,Y
AND	AND memory with accumulator.	IMM ABS ZPG (ABS,X) (ABS),Y ZPG,X ABS,X ABS,Y
ASL	Shift left one bit (memory or accumulator).	ABS ZPG ACC ZPG,X ABS,X
BCC	Branch on carry clear	REL
BCS	Branch on carry set.	REL
BEQ	Branch on result zero.	REL

Mnemonic code	Brief description	Addressing modes
BIT	Test bits in memory with accumulator	ABS ZPG
BMI	Branch on result minus.	REL
BNE	Branch on result not zero.	REL
BPL	Branch on result plus.	REL
BRK	Force break.	IMP
BVC	Branch on overflow clear.	REL
BVS	Branch on overflow set.	REL
CLC	Clear carry flag.	IMP
CLD	Clear decimal mode.	IMP
CLI	Clear interrupt disable bit.	IMP
CLV	Clear overflow flag.	IMP
CMP	Compare memory and accumulator	IMM ABS ZPG (ABS,X) (ABS),Y ZPG,X ABS,X ABS,Y
CPX	Compare memory and index X.	IMM ABS ZPG
CPY	Compare memory and index Y.	IMM ABS ZPG
DEC	Decrement memory by one.	ABS ZPG ZPG,X ABS,X
DEX	Decrement index X by one.	IMP
DEY	Decrement index Y by one.	IMP
EOR	Exclusive or memory with accumulator.	IMM ABS ZPG (ABS,X) (ABS),Y ZPG,X ABS,X ABS,Y
INC	Increment memory by one.	ABS ZPG ZPG,X ABS,X
INX	Increment index X by one.	IMP
INY	Increment index Y by one.	IMP
JMP	Jump to new location.	ABS IDR
JSR	Jump to new location saving return address.	ABS
LDA	Load accumulator with memory.	IMM ABS ZPG (ABS,X) (ABS),Y ZPG,X ABS,X ABS,Y
LDX	Load index X with memory.	IMM ABS ZPG ABS,Y ZPG,Y
LDY	Load index Y with memory.	IMM ABS ZPG ZPG,X ABS,X
LSR	Shift one bit right (memory or accumulator.	ABS ZPG ACC ZPG,X ABS,X

Mnemonic code	Brief description	Addressing modes
NOP	No operation.	IMP
ORA	OR memory with accumulator.	IMM ABS ZPG (ABS,X) (ABS),Y ZPG,X ABS,X ABS,Y
PHA	Push accumulator on stack.	IMP
PHP	Push processor status on stack.	IMP
PLA	Pull accumulator from stack.	IMP
PLP	Pull processor status from stack.	IMP
ROL	Rotate one bit left (memory or accumulator).	ABS ZPG ACC ZPG,X ABS,X
ROR	Rotate one bit right (memory or accumulator).	ABS ZPG ACC ZPG,X ABS,X
RTI	Return from interrupt.	IMP
RTS	Return from subroutine.	IMP
SBC	Subtract memory from accumulator with borrow.	IMM ABS ZPG (ABS,X) (ABS),Y ZPG,X ABS,X ABS,Y
SEC	Set carry flag.	IMP
SED	Set decimal mode.	IMP
SEI	Set interrupt disable status.	IMP
STA	Store accumulator in memory.	ABS ZPG (ABS,X) (ABS),Y ZPG,X ABS,X ABS,Y
STX	Store index X in memory.	ABS ZPG ZPG,Y
STY	Store index Y in memory.	ABS ZPG ZPG,X
TAX	Transfer accumulator to index X.	IMP
TAY	Transfer accumulator to index Y.	IMP
TSX	Transfer stack pointer to index X.	IMP
TXA	Transfer index X to accumulator.	IMP
TXS	Transfer index X to stack pointer.	IMP
TYA	Transfer index Y to accumulator.	IMP

Key to addressing modes:

IMM	Immediate	ZPG,X	Zero page, X indexed
ABS	Absolute	ZPG,Y	Zero page, Y indexed
ZPG	Zero page	ABS,X	X indexed
ACC	Accumulator	ABS,Y	X indexed
IMP	Implied	REL	Relative
(ABS,X)	Indexed indirect	IDR	Indirect
(ABS),Y	Indirect indexed		

Forward references – two-pass assembly

If you try the following short program:

```
10 DIM CODE% 10
20 P%=CODE%
30 [
40   LDA #0
50   BEQ EXIT
60   LDA #0
70  .EXIT LDA #0
80 ]
```

you will get an error message. The trouble doesn't lie in the program in the sense that there is nothing wrong with the code. It may not be very useful but it is correct. The trouble comes from the use of the label EXIT in line 50 before it has been defined in line 70. This is exactly the same problem as using a variable before it has been assigned in a BASIC program. The solution, however, is a little more difficult. You cannot move the definition of EXIT before line 50 for obvious reasons (it labels the position of the LDA instruction in line 70!). When you reach line 80 the label EXIT is defined. In fact, when you reach the closing bracket any labels used in the program are defined. If, at this point, the assembler is directed to have another go at converting the program to machine code, there is no longer a problem about labels not being defined. As labels are just standard BASIC variables they retain their definitions until the end of the BASIC program that the assembly language is part of. This use the assembler twice is known as *two-pass assembly*. To make the assembler examine the same assembly language twice all we need is a simple FOR loop. If you add:

```
15 FOR P=1 TO 2
```

and

```
85 NEXT P
```

then the assembly language will be assembled twice. Unfortunately, this simple method doesn't work because the program still gives an error message and stops when it reaches the first use of EXIT. What we need is some way of saying 'ignore errors and don't bother to produce a listing on the first pass through the program'. After all, the first pass through the program is simply collecting definitions of all the labels so why worry about any errors? If they are real errors they will still be there on the second pass. The assembler contains a command for just this purpose – OPT. There are four possible OPTions which have the following effects:

OPT 0 Ignore errors and don't produce a listing.
OPT 1 Ignore errors but list the program.
OPT 2 Report errors but not listing.
OPT 3 Report errors and produce a listing.

On the first pass we clearly want OPT 0 and on the second pass we want OPT 3. This is easy to arrange. Change the FOR loop in the program to read:

```
15 FOR P=0 TO 3 STEP 3
```

and change line 30 to

```
30 COPT P
```

This will cure the problem entirely! In general it is usual to use two-pass assembly with a listing produced on the second pass but once you have a working program there is no need to see the listing every time it is run so change OPT 3 to OPT 2. There are plenty of real examples of two-pass assembly in the next chapter.

Mixing BASIC and assembler

There is no problem with mixing BASIC and assembler with the BBC Micro. In fact we have been doing it from the very beginning of this chapter. However, in practice, mixing BASIC and assembler involves passing information between BASIC programs and assembly language programs and this requires a few more details.

There are two ways of calling an assembly language subroutine from BASIC – the USR function and the CALL statement.

The USR function is the best one to use if the assembly language program needs only a small number of values passed to it and needs to return only a small number of answers. The way that information is passed to the assembly language program is via the resident integer variables. The command USR(address) will transfer control to the machine code starting at the memory location at 'address'. Notice that 'address' can be a constant or a label. For example, USR(CODE%) is allowed. Following the USR statement and before the machine code is actually set running, the contents of A% are stored in the A register and likewise the contents of X% and Y% are stored in the registers of the same name. (In fact it is only the lower byte of these memory locations that is stored in the registers but this makes no difference as long as their contents are in the range 0 to 255.) In addition, the C flag in the P register is set to the least significant bit in the variable C%.

This is how information is passed to the machine code. How, then, is it passed back? The answer is that, like all functions, USR returns a single number as its result. This single number is made up of the contents of four of the machine's registers. USR returns a four byte integer and the contents of the registers are stored one to a byte in the order C, Y, X and A. The only problem in making any sense of this result is to separate them out. This is most easily done by using AND. If you want the contents of the A register as the result then, for example, use:

```
ANS=USR(CODE%) AND &00FF
```

which blanks out all the bytes of the answer except the least significant which contains the A register's value. The only thing that hasn't been mentioned is how to get back from assembler to BASIC. Both a USR function or a CALL statement transfer control to the machine code using a JSR instruction, so to return to BASIC simply use an RTS.

The CALL statement is similar to the USR function in that it transfers control to a machine code subroutine and transfers the contents of the resident integer variables A%,X%,Y% and C% to the corresponding registers or bits. However, instead of returning a single numerical answer it can return any number of answers of any type. It can also pass any variables to the machine code subroutine. The way that this works is rather complicated in that it involves the setting up of a *parameter block*. This is simply a list of machine addresses where the variables concerned are stored. Manipulation of BASIC variables from machine code needs a knowledge of how they are stored (see Chapter Two) and is not really within the scope of this chapter. The rules for using CALL with parameters are given in the User Guide and will not be repeated here.

There is an easy way to return limited information from both USR and CALL. The addresses at which the resident integer variables are stored were given in Chapter Two. Using this information, you can store any registers you like in these variables before returning to BASIC. An example of this technique will be found in Chapter Eight.

Conclusion

This chapter has been able to provide only an introduction to assembly language on the BBC Micro. After reading it you should have grasped the fundamental ideas of the instruction set, addressing modes, the registers and the BBC Micro's internal assembler. When you sit down to write your own assembly language programs, however, you will require further detailed information and will need to use a reference book about 6502 assembly language. It is worth repeating that the only way to learn assembly language is to use it. A number of examples is given in the next chapter along with more advanced ways of using the BBC Micro's assembler.

Chapter Eight
Assembly Language II

In this chapter the BBC Micro's assembler is examined in a little more detail. Some of its less obvious features will be discussed and illustrated by a number of short projects. These projects are complete in themselves but they are also intended to form the basis for your own experiments.

Labels and P%

Almost the whole story behind assembly language labels is contained in the statement that labels are just BASIC variables that are used to hold an address. However, the wider meanings of this observation are worth spelling out. There are two ways to set a variable equal to an address. You can use it to *label* a position in a program by writing its name preceded by a full stop (as described in the last chapter) or you can assign a value to it just like any other variable. Assigning an address to a label can be used to make assembly language programs easier to read and write. For example, instead of writing JSR &FFF4 to call OSBYTE (see Chapter Three) you can write

```
10 OSBYTE%=&FFF4
20 [ JSR OSBYTE%
   ...
```

While on the subject of storing addresses in variables, it is worth pointing out that you can use either real or integer variables to hold addresses but, of course, integer variables will make the assembler work slightly faster and will save storage space in the variables area of memory.

It is a fundamental principle of BASIC that anywhere that you can use a variable or a constant you can use an expression. For example, wherever you can write PRINT A, you can also write things like PRINT A*2+4. Unfortunately, not all versions of BASIC keep to this rule in all situations. BBC BASIC sticks to it almost without exception. (You cannot use expressions in place of the constants in *FX commands but these are implemented by the MOS, not by BASIC). Labels are no exception to this general rule and so anywhere you can use a label you can use an expression. For example,

LDA #ASC("A") Loads the A register with the ASCII code for the letter A.

STA DATA+2   Store the contents of the A register in the memory location whose address is the result of DATA+2.

If you want to load a 16-bit value then it has to be split into two bytes, an MSB and a LSB. This can be done very easily using the MOD and DIV functions. For example:

LDX (DATA% MOD 256)   loads X with the LSB

and

LDY (DATA% DIV 256)   loads Y with the MSB

The ability to use expressions to work out addresses in the assembler is very useful. It should be remembered, however, that the expressions are evaluated when the assembly language is being assembled into machine code, and not when the machine code program is run.

The resident integer variable P% has already been discussed in the previous chapter in the context of setting the start address of the memory into which the machine code is loaded. However, P% can be used for much more than just this. The value stored in P% is continually changing during the assembly so as to always hold the address of the memory location that the next byte of machine code will be stored in. Thus, at the end of a successful assembly, P% points to the first memory location after the machine code program. You should now be able to see that the definition of a label using a full stop is the same as setting it equal to the value of P%. In other words:

```
100   [
110     LDA DATR
120  .LABEL STR DATA+1
130     JMP LOOP
```

is the same as

```
100 [
110   LDA DATA ]
120 LABEL=P%
130 [
140 STA DATA+1
150 JMP LOOP ]
```

Notice that it is necessary to leave the assembler to set the variable 'LABEL' equal to 'P%'. (This idea of leaving assembler in the middle of a program, using some BASIC and returning to the program is useful in itself and will be discussed later.) Not only can the value of P% be assigned to other variables, it can also be altered. For example, if you want to use a few memory locations in the middle of a program to store data then you can leave assembler, increase the value of P% by the number of bytes you require and then return to assembler. If you want to refer to the memory locations by name then all you have to do is set up labels equal to intermediate values of P%. For example, if you want to use three memory locations for data storage and call them DATA1, DATA2 and DATA3 all you have to do is:

```
    assembly language
]
  DATA1=P%
  DATA2=P%+1
  DATA3=P%+2
  P%=P%+3
  [
assembly language continued
```

The line numbers have been left out for clarity. You can use indirection operators to set initial values in memory locations used for data. You could add ?DATA1=33 to the last example if you wanted the memory location whose address was stored in DATA1 to be initialised to 33.

Getting results to and from assembly language subroutines

The idea of passing values to assembly language subroutine using the resident integer variables was discussed in the previous chapter. The USR function caters for the need to return a few simple values but it can involve the use of messy expressions with AND and DIV to separate the different parts of the result. A cleaner, though nonstandard method, is to use the information presented in Chapter Two concerning the locations of the resident integer variables to store results into them directly. You can see an example of this method in Project 2.

For more complicated situations there is really no choice but to use the parameter-passing facility of the CALL statement. Following a CALL with parameters, information is stored starting at &600 as to the type and location of each parameter. This information can be used by assembly language programs to 'collect' data from or store results in BASIC variables. The details of this are straightforward and as there is an example given in the User Guide the subject will not be discussed further.

Using memory

Reserving memory for assembly language subroutines and data seems to be no problem on the BBC Micro. However, there are two instances where the usual DIM statement method of reserving memory is inadequate. The first case is when you want to 'hide' a machine code program in RAM so that other programs can be written without having to worry about the machine code while still having it available for use. An example of this problem will be found in Project 1 where a screen dump program is written. Ideally this program should be stored in an area of memory that isn't used by a BASIC program and one of the function keys set to produce the string CALL 'address'|M where 'address' is the start address of the screen dump program. This would allow the screen dump program to be loaded before any other BASIC program and be called into action by pressing the function key. There are several places where machine code can be 'tucked away' but none of them is particularly satisfactory. For example, you can lower the value in HIMEM and store the machine code just below the screen memory. The trouble is that changing modes changes the value of HIMEM, possibly destroying the machine code. However, if you can ensure that a MODE statement will not be used, then altering HIMEM is a possibility. A much better way of hiding machine code is to alter PAGE but this is more difficult because the program that creates the machine code must be loaded and RUN AFTER the PAGE has been altered. For more details see Project 1.

The second situation where DIM is insufficient concerns the allocation of memory for data storage. Locations in page zero are particularly important to the 6502. For example, the only way that you can specify a variable 16-bit address is by using:

```
LDY #0
LDA (ADDRESS),Y
```

where ADDRESS holds the address of the first of two page zero locations. The effect of this pair of instructions is to load the A register from the location whose address is stored in the two page zero memory locations. In this way pairs of memory locations in page zero can be used as '16-bit pointers' to other memory locations. For this reason the BBC Micro sets aside page zero locations from &70 to &8F for user routines. Page zero locations are in short supply so use somewhere else unless you really *need* page zero.

Conditional assembly and macros

One of the great advantages of having a 6502 assembler as part of BASIC is that you can make use of all of the BASIC statements in the translation of a program to machine code. For example, if you wanted to write a machine code subroutine that was to be used for a number of purposes and each purpose required a slightly different version, then you could use an IF statement to select which version was actually assembled. To illustrate this, consider the problem of setting the transmission speed of a communications program (see Project 2.) You could use something like:

```
IF FAST=1 THEN [ LDA #600:] ELSE [ LDA #300:]
```

where FAST is a normal BASIC variable that controls which of the two assembly language statements is translated into the machine code program. Notice that the IF is only carried out when the assembly language is being converted to machine code. It is *not* part of the resulting machine code program. (The colon before the] can be used instead of a carriage return to end an assembly language statement. In fact the colon can be used to put multiple statements on one line just as in BASIC!)

This selective assembly is a powerful tool and makes the BBC Micro's simple assembler look more like a complex *macro assembler*. As another example, suppose you needed to carry out the same operation ROR A a number of times. Instead of writing it out each time, why not use:

```
FOR I=1 TO 4
[ ROR A
]
NEXT I
```

which will include four ROR A instructions in any assembly language program that it is part of. The best way to understand what each of these examples does is to type them in with some other assembly language and see what appears on the listing.

Finally, it is worth pointing out the BBC assembler coupled with BBC BASIC provides a full macro facility! A macro is like a subroutine except that it produces the necessary assembly language each time it is called. Once again, it is easier to understand this idea by means of an example. It is often necessary to add the contents of two memory locations together and store the answer in a third. The following 'macro' generates assembly language to do just this:

```
DEF PROCADD(N1,N2,ANS)
[ CLC
   LDA N1
   ADC N2
   STA ANS
]
ENDPROC
```

To add the two numbers in DATA1 and DATA2 and store the answer in DATA3 you would simply write:

```
PROCADD(DATA1,DATA2,DATA3)
```

This would generate the correct assembly language at the position at which it was used. You can use PROCADD as many times as you like in a program. A new copy of the assembly language will be produced each time. You can even use local labels within a macro simply by naming them in a LOCAL statement! The possibilities are endless!

Project 1 - a text screen dump program

The object of this project is to write a screen dump program. A general screen dump program would be capable of printing whatever was displayed on the screen in any mode. This includes attempting to give a representation of the colours used as a grey scale! This is not an easy task and it is not possible to tackle the problem in general because the solution depends on which of the many graphics printers is available. To make the problem a little easier and as a starting point for more advanced programs we will only try to dump mode 7 text screens.

There are many ways of approaching the problem of writing a mode 7 screen dump program. At first thought it might seem like a good idea to use the screen memory map to retrieve the ASCII code stored in each screen location and send them to the printer in turn. However, this method becomes very difficult if the screen has scrolled because of the increased complexity of the memory map. Rather than have to live with a 'no scroll' restriction it is better to use the MOS subroutine OSBYTE called with A=135. This returns the ASCII code of the character under the text cursor's current position. Once we have decided to use this OSBYTE call, the other problems within the program are:

1. Sending characters to the printer only.
2. 'Scanning' the text cursor across the screen.
3. Sending carriage returns at the end of each line full off the screen.

Each of these problems is also solved with the help of an MOS call. The resulting program is:

```
 10 DIM MACH% 150
 20 OSBYTE%=&FFF4
 30 OSWRCH%=&FFEE
 40 OSASCI%=&FFE3
 50 XCORD%=MACH%
 60 YCORD%=MACH%+1
 70 CODE%=MACH%+2
 80 PROCASMB
 90 CLS
100 FOR I=1 TO 24
110 PRINT "TEST OUTPUT ",I
120 NEXT I
130 CALL CODE%
140 STOP

150 DEF PROCASMB
160 FOR PASS=0 TO 3 STEP 3
170 P%=CODE%
180 COPT PASS

190 LDA #5
200 LDX #1
210 JSR OSBYTE%
220 LDX #0
230 STX XCORD%
240 STX YCORD%
250 .SCAN% LDA #31
```

```
260 JSR OSWRCH%
270 LDA XCORD%
280 JSR OSWRCH%
290 LDA YCORD%
300 JSR OSWRCH%
310 JSR DUMP
320 LDX XCORD%
330 INX
340 STX XCORD%
350 CPX #32
360 BNE SCAN%
370 LDX #0
380 STX XCORD%
390 LDX #&0D
400 JSR PRN
410 LDX YCORD%
420 INX
430 STX YCORD%
440 CPX #25
450 BNE SCAN%
460 RTS

470 .DUMP LDA #135
480 JSR OSBYTE%
490 JSR PRN
500 RTS

510 .PRN LDA #2
520 JSR OSWRCH%
530 LDA #21
540 JSR OSWRCH%
550 TXA
560 JSR OSWRCH%
570 LDA #6
580 JSR OSWRCH%
590 LDA #3
600 JSR OSWRCH%
610 RTS
620 ]

630 NEXT PASS
640 ENDPROC
```

The first few lines (10 to 70) set up the area of memory that the machine code will be stored in and the values of some labels that will be used later. Notice the way that two memory locations are reserved for data storage by lines 50,60 and 70 – the start of the machine code is stored in CODE%. The main program calls PROCASMB to assemble the dump subroutine to machine code and then prints some test lines on the screen before calling it in line 130. The assembly language dump routine can be seen in line 190 to 620. The rest of PROCASMB implements two passes over the assembly language as described in Chapter Seven. The first part of the machine code 190 to 210 sets up a parallel printer as described in the User Guide using the OSBYTE equivalent of *FX 5,1. Lines 220 and 240 initialise the data locations XCORD% and YCORD% to zero to start the scan of every location on the screen. XCORD% is used to hold the *x* co-ordinate and YCORD% is used to hold the *y* co-ordinate of the text cursor. Lines 250 to 300 use the VDU drivers via OSWRCH to set the cursor to the position stored in XCORD% and YCORD%. Line 300 calls a machine code subroutine DUMP which sends the character under the cursor to the printer (details given later). The rest of the program, from 320 to 460, is concerned with moving the cursor over the screen by updating XCORD% and YCORD%. After each character is dumped to the printer, XCORD% has one added to it (lines 320 to 340) and it is then compared with 32 to see if we have reached the end of a screen line. If we have, then XCORD% is set to zero (lines 370 and 380), a carriage return is sent to the printer to start a new line (lines 390 and 400) and YCORD% has one added to it to take the cursor down one line (lines 410 to 430). At this point YCORD% is compared to 25 (line 440). If it is equal to 25 then all the lines have been dumped and the subroutine ends (line 500). The only things left to explain are the two subroutines DUMP and PRN. DUMP uses the OSBYTE call discussed earlier to get the ASCII code of the character under the cursor into the X register (lines 470 and 480). It then calls subroutine PRN which sends the character in the X register to the printer only. Subroutine PRN starts by turning the printer on with the equivalent of a VDU 2 command (lines 510 and 520). It then disables the VDU drivers so that the character only goes to the printer using the equivalent of VDU 21 (lines 530 and 550). The character is then sent to the printer using OSWRCH (line 550 and 560). The remainder of the subroutine enables the VDU drivers (lines 570 and 580) and then disables the printer (lines 590 and 600).

There is one last part to this project. The dump subroutine is only really useful if it can be in memory at the same time as any BASIC program – not just the one that produces it. This can be done by first saving the whole dump on tape. Then type NEW and type PRINT ~PAGE and write down the answer. Then alter PAGE by typing PAGE=PAGE+&100. This moves the start of any BASIC program &100 memory locations higher up and leaves space for the machine code. Now load the dump program from tape and alter line 10 to read MACH%= 'the old value of PAGE' (which you wrote down earlier). Also delete the test section of the main program, lines

90–130. RUN the program and then delete it using NEW. You can now load and run any other BASIC program you like and obtain a screen dump by typing CALL 'the old value of PAGE +2'. You can even program a function key to produce the same command and hence dump the screen with a single key stroke!

This program can be easily adapted to dump text from any mode screen by simply changing the values to which XCORD% and YCORD% are compared to detect the end of line and the end of screen respectively. You can even go on to expand the program to dump graphics by using the OSWORD call that returns the value of a single point on the screen but this is more complicated!!

Project 2 – a VDU program

The next project is likely to be of interest only to people with access to another computer because it turns the BBC micro into a VDU. The principle behind this is straightforward and is based on the description of the RS423 interface given in Chapter One. This project is a good example of how BASIC and assembly language can be used together. The program is split into a number of small subroutines. INIT% initialises the ACIA and the serial controller. CHAROUT% sends a character stored in the X register to the ACIA transmit register. CHAREADY checks to see if there is a character in the receive register. It returns its result by storing the A register in the first byte of the resident integer variable A% at &0404. CHARGET% retrieves the character in the receive register. It, too, returns its result through A%. Using these three subroutines and a little BASIC, the entire VDU program can be written:

```
 10 DIM INIT% 20
 20 DIM CHAROUT% 20
 30 DIM CHAREADY% 20
 40 DIM CHARGET% 20
 50 SERCON%=&FE10
 60 ACIACON%=&FE08
 70 ACIASTAT%=&FE08
 80 ACIATRAN%=&FE09
 90 ACIAREC%=&FE09
100 GOSUB 130
110 CALL INIT%
120 GOSUB 490
```

```
130 FOR S=0 TO 3 STEP 3

140 P%=INIT%
150 COPT S
160   LDA #&13
170   STA ACIACON%
180   LDA #&56
190   STA ACIACON%
200   LDA #&49
210   STA SERCON%
220   RTS
230 ]

240 P%=CHAROUT%
250 COPT S
260 .OUT1 LDA ACIASTAT%
270   AND #&0A
280   BEQ OUT1
290   STX ACIATRAN%
300   RTS
310 ]

320 P%=CHAREADY%
330 COPT S
340   LDA ACIACON%
350   AND #&01
360   STA &0404
370   RTS
380 ]

390 P%=CHARGET%
400 COPT S
410   LDA ACIAREC%
420   AND #&7F
430   STA &0404
440   RTS
450 ]

460 NEXT S
470 RETURN

480 REM VDU LOOP
490 X%=INKEY(0)
500 IF X%=-1 THEN GOTO 520
510 CALL CHAROUT%
520 CALL CHAREADY%
530 IF A%=0 THEN GOTO 490
540 CALL CHARGET%
550 PRINT CHR$(A%);
560 GOTO 490
```

The machine subroutines that make up this program have already been described briefly and should cause no trouble. INIT% sets the baud rate to 1200 baud but this can easily be changed using the information given in Chapter One. However, notice the alternative way of writing a set of assembly language subroutines using a separate area for each. The main program starts at 490 and forms an infinite loop that can only be broken by pressing ESCAPE or BREAK. Line 490 reads the keyboard to see if a key is being pressed. If one is, then the ASCII code in X% is sent to CHAROUT%. If no key is pressed, CHAREADY% is called to see if there is a character in the receive register. If there is, it is retrieved by CHARGET (line 540) and printed by line 550.

This program is really only the basis for a full VDU program. It should give the user the option of selecting any baud rate, parity etc., in an extended initialisation section. However, the program given here does illustrate how assembly language and BASIC can be used together and how the resident integer variables can be used to transfer information.

Project 3 - a moving graphics program

This book would not be complete without a moving graphics program and Project 3 is just that. It forms the basis for a 'squash'-type program. A square graphics character CHR$(224) is bounced around the screen. Because it is written in assembly language this program gives you an idea of just how fast graphics can be on the BBC Micro.

```
 10 MODE 4
 20 DIM MACH% 300
 30 VDU 23,224,&FF,&FF,&FF,&FF,&FF,&FF,&FF,&FF
 40 PROCASME
 50 PROCPLAY
 60 STOP

 70 DEF PROCASME
 80 OSWRCH%=&FFEE
 90 OSBYTE%=&FFF4
100 XCORD%=MACH%
110 YCORD%=MACH%+1
120 XVEL%=MACH%+2
130 YVEL%=MACH%+3
140 CODE%=MACH%+4
150 ?XVEL%=1
160 ?YVEL%=-1
```

```
170 FOR PASS=0 TO 3 STEP 3
180 P%=CODE%
190 COPT PASS

200 STX XCORD%
210 STY YCORD%
220 .LOOP JSR SHOW%
230 JSR MOV%
240 JSR BOUNCE%
250 JSR DELAY%
260 JMP LOOP

270 .SHOW% LDA #8
280 JSR OSWRCH%
290 LDA #32
300 JSR OSWRCH%
310 LDA #31
320 JSR OSWRCH%
330 LDA XCORD%
340 JSR OSWRCH%
350 LDA YCORD%
360 JSR OSWRCH%
370 LDA #224
380 JSR OSWRCH%
390 RTS

400 .MOV% LDA XCORD%
410 CLC
420 ADC XVEL%
430 STA XCORD%
440 LDA YCORD%
450 CLC
460 ADC YVEL%
470 STA YCORD%
480 RTS

490 .BOUNCE% LDA XCORD%
500 CMP #1
510 BEQ FLIPX%
520 CMP #39
530 BNE YBON%
540 .FLIPX% LDA #0
550 SEC
560 SBC XVEL%
570 STA XVEL%
580 .YBON% LDA YCORD%
590 CMP #1
600 BEQ FLIPY%
610 CMP #31
620 BNE FIN%
630 .FLIPY% LDA #0
640 SEC
650 SBC YVEL%
```

```
660 STA YVEL%
670 .FIN% RTS

680 .DELAY% LDA #19
690 JSR OSBYTE%
700 RTS

710 ]
720 NEXT PASS
730 ENDPROC

740 DEF PROCPLAY
750 CLS
760 VDU 23,1,0;0;0;0;
770 X%=RND(15)
780 Y%=RND(5)+10
790 CALL CODE%
800 ENDPROC
```

The main program calls PROCASMB to produce the machine code used by PROCPLAY to bounce the ball around the screen. There are four assembly language subroutines within PROCASMB – MOV% moves the ball, BOUNCE% makes sure that the ball doesn't go off the screen, SHOW% updates the ball's position on the screen and DELAY% slows things down so that the ball can be seen! PROCPLAY turns off the cursor (line 760) and sets the starting position for the ball at random (lines 770 and 780) before calling the machine code (line 790). The first thing the machine code does is to use X and Y to initialise XCORD% and YCORD% to the starting position. The main loop within the program calls SHOW%, MOV%, BOUNCE% and DELAY% repeatedly (lines 220 to 260). SHOW% is straightforward and uses the equivalent of VDU 31 to move the cursor to the new position (lines 290 to 360). It then prints the ball character using OSWRCH (lines 370 to 390). The only difficult part of the subroutine occurs at the start, where lines 270 to 300 move the cursor back one place and print a blank (ASCII code 32) to remove the old ball's position. The MOV% subroutine updates the X and Y co-ordinates in XCORD% and YCORD% by adding the contents of XVEL% and YVEL% respectively. Notice how these data bytes are initialised in lines 150 and 160. BOUNCE% is the most complicated subroutine, but all it does is to check to see if the new co-ordinates are on the edge of the screen or not. If they are it reverses one of the velocities contained in XVEL% or YVEL%. Reversing a velocity is done by subtracting it from zero (lines 540 to 570 and 630 to 660). DELAY% is a very simple subroutine and merely carries out the equivalent of an *FX 19. This halts the program until the start of the NEXT TV frame. This means that the ball can only move every fiftieth of a second. If you want to see how fast the ball can really move just remove line 250!

You should be able to add a bat to the ball bouncing routine without too much trouble and have one of the fastest squash games ever!

Project 4 – a pulse generator

The final project is more hardware-oriented than the previous three. The BBC Micro contains so many timers that an obvious technical application is to use it as a general purpose pulse generator. Project 4 is a simple pulse generator that can produce a square wave out of PB7. A second purpose behind this project is to illustrate some of the information given about the timers in Chapter Six.

The program consists of three parts – an assembly language subroutine that sets the registers in VIA-B to the appropriate values, a BASIC procedure PROCPULSE that uses the machine code to program the VIA, and a main program. The main program first assembles the assembly language by calling PROCASMB and then reads in PL% and calls PROCPULSE to set the period and start the train of square waves coming out of PB7.

```
  10 DIM CODE% 100
  20 PROCASMB
  30 INPUT PL%
  40 PROCPULSE(PL%)
  50 GOTO 30
  60 STOP

  70 DEF PROCASMB
  80 AUXC%=&FE6B
  90 T1CLL%=&FE64
 100 T1CH%=&FE65
 110 IRQC%=&FE6E
 120 P%=CODE%
 130 FOR PASS=0 TO 3 STEP 3
 140 [OPT PASS

 150 LDA #&40
 160 STA IRQC%
 170 LDA AUXC%
 180 ORA #&C0
 190 STA AUXC%
 200 STX T1CLL%
 210 STY T1CH%
```

```
220 RTS
230 ]

240 NEXT PASS
250 ENDPROC

260 DEF PROCPULSE(PERIOD%)
270 X%=PERIOD% MOD 256
280 Y%=PERIOD% DIV 256
290 CALL CODE%
300 ENDPROC
```

Notice once again the different way of forming the machine code by calling PROCASMB which contains the definitions of all the labels used by the machine code. It is a good idea, however, to leave the DIM statement that reserves memory at the start of the entire program so that it is easy to find. The machine code subroutine first disables any interrupts that timer 1 might try to produce (lines 150 to 160). It then sets up timer 1 in the free running mode with PB7 enabled by storing the correct control bits in the auxiliary control register (line 170 to 190). Finally, it stores the X register into the low order latch and the Y register into the high order counter/latch which starts the counter off. The procedure PROCPULSE (PERIOD%) simply divides the value in PERIOD% into a low byte and a high byte and stores them in X% and Y% respectively. When you run the program, the value that you give to PL% will determine the width of each pulse in the square wave in microseconds. Once a pulse train is started it may be altered by entering a different value of PL%. You might be surprised, however, to discover that the pulses carry on after the program has been stopped by pressing ESCAPE!

Conclusion

This second chapter on the BBC Micro's assembly language builds on the information presented in Chapter Seven. It contains four projects which between them cover many aspects of machine code programming. The BBC Micro's facility for combining BASIC and assembly language is an attractive feature which is explored via two of these practical examples. A useful philosophy for writing software on the BBC Micro is to use BASIC wherever possible and resort to assembly language when necessary to speed things up or to add commands to the system.

Chapter Nine
Postscript

Nobody who has read the rest of this book will have missed the fact that I am an unashamed admirer of the BBC Micro. As far as I am concerned it is at the top of its league and rightly so. The factor that makes it stand out from other currently available home computers is its overall design concept.

Even the BBC Micro Model A has a very impressive specification for a microcomputer. When expanded to the Model B it is one of the most capable and sophisticated machines on the market. However, the expansion doesn't stop at the Model B. A quick look inside to see all the unfilled spaces on the printed circuit board soon confirms this. The BBC Micro is not just a brilliantly designed microcomputer, it is the start of a complete system. There is provision on the printed circuit board for a disc interface, a speech synthesiser, an Econet interface and a removable ROM pack.

With all this *on-board* expansion it is easy to miss the overall unity behind the design of the BBC Micro system. For example, the standard Model A and B machine, just like most small micros, uses a cassette recorder to provide a backing store. However, the BBC Micro uses the tape recorder as only one of a number of *filing systems* whereas other micros use completely different ways of dealing with different forms of backing store. When you add a new piece of equipment, such as a disc or an Econet interface, you not only have to install the necessary chips, you also have to provide new filing system software in the form of additional paged ROMs. You can select one of the possible filing systems by using MOS commands such as *TAPE,*DISC or even *NET for the Econet filing system.

There are other extras that can be used with the BBC Micro apart from the on-board circuits. The mysterious *tube* has already been mentioned in Chapter One as a way of connecting another CPU to the system. The two add-on processors available at the time of writing are remarkable in themselves. A 3 MHz 6502 processor board will be capable of running programs even faster than the 2 MHz 6502 in the BBC machine itself – and the BBC machine already has a reputation for being a very fast machine. The Z80 card can run CP/M programs with a much larger amount of user RAM than is normally available in a CP/M system because the BBC Micro takes care of all the disc and other I/O handling. If these two extra processors weren't enough, the promised 16-bit processor should bring large computer performance to the microcomputer world.

You may feel that using the BBC Micro as nothing more than a graphics VDU to a second processor is a waste of hardware. This is far from the truth. Most of the cost of a micro lies in the video display, the keyboard and all the other peripherals. The microprocessor itself and the RAM are rapidly becoming very cheap commodities and using the BBC Micro as an 'environment' in which other microprocessors can work is a very sensible arrangement. Acorn have been clever enough to find a way of interfacing these second processors over a fast and well-defined interface – the tube.

For technical and laboratory situations, it is worth knowing that the 1 MHz bus can be used to connect the original Acorn range of 'Eurocard' modules. This is particularly useful when a wide range of extra digital and analog interfaces are required. It is also particularly easy to build your own cards to work from the 1 MHz bus. This is more than can be said for the tube which needs a special Acorn-designed ULA. With its speed, graphics and internal interfaces, the BBC Micro is an ideal scientific machine (and any machine that is a good general scientific machine is a good business machine!)

This book has tended to stress the BBC Micro as an isolated computer. The reason for this has been the need to keep to a reasonable length! Even the on-board expansion – for example, the disc system and speech synthesiser – has been neglected to make room for a discussion of standard Model A/B features. The problem about starting to discuss the BBC Micro's expansion capabilities is that they are vast. Each of the pieces of equipment mentioned in the previous few paragraphs deserves at least one chapter to itself and that's just the start of the list of possible extras. To it we already need to add the Prestel interface and the Teletext add-on. In some ways it is premature to write about the BBC Micro's expansion modules – at the time of writing not all of them are available in the sense of being on the market, although I have seen all of them (apart from the 16-bit second processor) in pre-production form. More importantly, it would be misleading for me to select which are the vital interfaces for inclusion in this final chapter. The interfaces that *you* will choose to expand *your* system will depend entirely on the purposes you want your BBC Micro to serve. Not everybody will want a disc drive or even a printer. Certainly, lots of BBC Micro systems will be complete without an Econet interface. Prestel and Teletext are currently billed as being important to every home in the future, but whether this prediction comes true remains to be seen. The 'home information' age has, however, arrived with the advent of the BBC Micro!

The only real way to appreciate the full implications of the BBC Micro's role as the heart of an expandable system is to study a few of the add-ons and see how they fit into the existing machine. For myself, this is certainly what I intend to do – and having done so will be in a proper position to write, not just a chapter, but a complete book about The BBC Micro System.

Index

A to D convertor, 93–107
ACIA, 9
adding commands, 48
addressing modes, 124–152
ADVAL, 99
analog, 98
arrays, 37
assembly language, 115

BASIC format, 31
BREAK key, 15

CALL, 124, 134–5
cassette, 7
character generator, 56
character table, 65
chords, 80
colour, 58
conditional assembley, 141
CPU, 2

digital, 97
disc interface, 153

Econet, 153
ENVELOPE, 83
ESCAPE key, 47
Eurocard modules, 154
events, 52

fire buttons, 100
functions, 23, 27, 37

garbage collection, 40

handshake lines, 104, 107
heap, 32
heap dump program, 38
hexadecimal, 29–30
HIMEM, 31

indirection, 29
instruction set, 130
interfaces, 6
interfacing, 96
integer variable, 35
interrupts, 49

joystick, 101–102

keyboard, 13

label, 123, 136
language work area, 31
local, 25, 42
LOCAL, 26, 42
LOMEM, 32

macros, 141
memory map, 19–20, 31
mode 7, 74
MOS, 43
MOS indirection, 45

NEW, 33

OLD, 33
OSBYTE, 45
OSWORD, 45

PAGE, 32
page zero, 31
paging, 3
palette, 69
parameters, 25
PEEKing the screen, 64
Prestel interface, 154
procedure, 23, 26–7, 37

real variable, 36
recursion, 28

registers, 128
resident integer variable, 40
RS243, 7

screen dump, 142
screen memory map, 55, 59–64
scrolling, 72
second processor, 154
serial control register, 12
serialiser, 69
shift register, 112
side effects, 26
soft machine, 43
SOUND, 77
sound effects, 82
sound generator, 76, 89
sound queue, 79
speech synthesiser, 153
stack, 32
string indirection, 30
string variable, 37
structured programming, 22
subroutine, 23

Teletext add-ons, 154
Teletext graphics, 74
timers, 109

tokens, 33
TOP, 32
transducer, 97, 101, 103
Tube, 17, 154
tunes, 79
two-pass assembly, 133

user port connections, 104
USR, 134

variable format, 34
variable storage, 34
VIA, 13, 104
video, 4, 49, 54
video generator, 4, 67
video processor, 4, 67
voltage divider, 102

1 MHz bus, 15, 154
6502, 2, 115
?, 29
!, 30
$, 30
&, 30
~, 30
*FX, 46